SELLING PUBLIC HEALTH

The no B.S. sales and marketing guide for local health departments struggling to stay relevant in today's world of epic competition and slashed budgets.

By Rick Reynolds

Copyright

Selling Public Health - *The no B.S. sales and marketing guide for local health departments struggling to stay relevant in today's world of epic competition and slashed budgets.*

Selling Public Health

The no B.S. sales and marketing guide for local health departments struggling to stay relevant in today's world of epic competition and slashed budgets.

Table of Contents

Forward

In July 1999 I was asked by a telephone interconnect owner if I would be willing to help a customer of his by setting them up with our on-hold marketing program.

When he said it was a public health department, I thought it was interesting that a health department would want to do something so progressive.

Although I was skeptical, I agreed to meet with the administrator and have a conversation to see if we could help.

When I arrived at the health department, the first thing that struck me was how professional all the staff seemed. Sure, the outer waiting room had young mothers and obese people who I thought looked needy, the kind of people who use a health department. But upon entering a third floor conference room, I was seated and about to get a real education.

The administrator and I greeted each other and I shared with her that this intitial meeting was not going to be a typical sales call, but more of a brief conversation so we could discover if we had a fit. As we asked and answered each other's questions, I began to learn some things that were surprising.

First, was that there was a lot more to a health department than I ever dreamed. I thought health departments just gave shots and maybe birth control. I had no idea how uninformed I was (and I grew up in a family where my maternal grandfather was a doctor and most of my family was involved in medicine).

The thing that truly shocked me was when I asked the administrator what she needed help with, she told me, "If I walked out on the street in front of this health department and asked people at random what we do here, nobody knows! They may be able to list one or two services, but most don't even know we exist!"

Thus began my foray and ultimate focus on how to help public health attract, inform, sell and resell their services to the community.

Once we helped the first health department, other counties in the same state heard about the success they had achieved and began calling and asking for our services at their local health departments.

This tidal wave of interest led me to attend our first National Association of City and County Health Officers (NACCHO) conference. While at a luncheon, I sat with several state directors of health as we shared information. I learned that the lack of proper marketing for public health is an epidemic of its' own. It is nationwide and not getting any better.

I learned that there are two ways public health markets itself: 1) A Public Information Officer (P.I.O.) or 2)

Someone on the staff *(usually untrained)* who was picked to become a marketing person.

Unfortunately, most picked for these positions have no background in generating traffic to the health department, no sales background and no knowledge of how to create a marketing plan. Even worse, most do not have systems in place to track the success (or failure) of their efforts.

Another thing I learned is that there is no continuity between public health departments–not just from state to state but also from county to county within a state. This disconnect is troubling but fixable.

Messages created by public health for mass consumption differ from messages created for a target market. So does the type of delivery. Marketing public health is a field full of many holes and inconsistencies that are as different as one health department from another.

An experienced health department director once shared with me the funny but accurate line, "Once you've seen one county health department, you've seen one county health department."

Messages created for the sake of cross-promotion and education will differ from messages created to save lives during a public health emergency situation, such as bio-terrorism or an epidemic like H1N1.

That is why I wrote this book. I want to provide readers with some of the tools and real life examples to show how many are failing and how some are doing it right.

I will highlight examples of the disconnect that I have personally experienced, as we have communicated with and helped health departments throughout the United States.

This book is meant to be a succinct guide to discovering new ways of thinking about how to increase the public's awareness of your services and programs. In it you will find an A to Z list of fresh ideas that my clients have used to experience quantum growth in their health departments. You will find my writing style is direct and conversational. With a commitment to overcoming your marketing shortfalls, follow my methods and you too will be a master at Selling Public Health!

Chapter 1 – The Beginning

Back when I first began in business-to-business sales, I learned how vital it was to stay abreast of all the possible ways to generate interest and sales for a particular product. As the years went by and my entrepreneurial spirit began to develop, I quickly rose up the ladder from sales to national sales director to owner of multiple sales companies.

In the early '90s at the advent of the Internet, I co-founded one of the first Internet marketing firms in the world that specialized in not only webpage design, but also secure online credit card transactions.

As often is the case, I was guided quite by accident into the field I have enjoyed for over 20 years: the field of marketing.

While some think of marketing as a static one-time advertisement, I always thought of it as a morphing, adjustable approach that should be able to reinvent itself in the moment.

One of the mediums I saw as being virtually untapped, and yet horribly managed, was the company telephone system. To me, it made no sense to spend thousands of dollars on advertisements, a pretty building and even nice furnishings if your phones were answered unprofessionally.

What I discovered was that most companies put the lowest paid, least qualified person on the front lines. This person had the huge responsibility of creating the public image that was going to make or break the first impression in the ears of the caller.

I also discovered that less than one percent of American businesses had some form of on-hold marketing or messages. Those that did often had a radio station playing or worse, commercials for their competition!

This sparked my interest to find out how we could provide specialized marketing services to our clients by using their telephone system. It would have to be done in a way that enabled us to control the content of their messages remotely and update them in a moment's notice when they needed to be changed (such as during a public health emergency).

What we came up with were multiple delivery options for our customers that enabled us to provide among other things, messages on-hold, day and night answer, preemptive messages and even call tracking.

Fast forward years later when I walked into that first health department and discovered the same lackluster approach to marketing and misguided staff answering and managing telephone calls.

Amazingly enough, I discovered more reasons that a health department could utilize our service. This came when a hurricane was barreling towards some of our Florida health departments and they went into emergency management mode.

With the approaching storm and the order for people to evacuate, one health department was converting into a special needs shelter later that afternoon. We were able to update their messages to inform callers so staff could prepare the health department, themselves and their families. This was made possible by the fact that we developed equipment that allowed us to change the messages callers heard remotely from our offices (far removed from the storm).

Now the writing was on the wall. We could help public health departments sell and promote their services, increase traffic and educate the community, all while providing a rapid response method of changing their messages during an emergency.

After September 11, 2001, everything changed. Although our clients made major inroads towards being effective marketers, the new battle cry was threat preparedness. This was one of those times when the world caught up with our technology. We had this covered as we had been providing up-to-date message changes to our clients for years.

With the myriad of challenges that were to occur from 2000-2010, our threat preparedness service was put to the test numerous times assisting our health department clients with emergency messages during hurricanes, floods, H1N1 outbreaks, flu vaccine shortages, the BP Oil spill, earthquakes, TB outbreaks and foodborne illness.

Although we could provide emergency message updates, and that was the new focus for public health, I still thought it was important to keep our eyes on marketing their services.

When the economic meltdown of 2008 started manifesting, I knew it was only a matter of time before public health would see shrinking budgets and increased pressure to perform with less.

A funny thing happens during a downturn; most people panic, cut back, do less, worry and shrivel while a select few see opportunities they never thought existed. While some health department administrators were planning their exit, others were realizing that economic downturn equals more people needing the services of the local health department. As [1]Winston Churchill once said, "This was their finest hour!" *(ref-1)*

Today, I hear the same things I have heard from the beginning of my journey of helping public health. I hear that nobody knows what the health department does. I still hear that there are a myriad of programs and services that might fade away due to lack of awareness

---

[1] *Ref 1*

and use. I don't hear so much about emergency preparedness anymore.

I believe that now is the time for each city, county and state to develop a plan to effectively utilize every tool at their disposal. From using their voicemail to messages on-hold, the Internet, social media, print, billboards, radio and outreach. This is the time to get serious and sell public health!

In this book, I will outline proven methods of marketing your health department. Some of this may sound crazy. Some may think, "This won't work for us." If you are that kind of person, you may want to stop reading now.

On the other hand, if you are open-minded and committed to cracking the code, this book will show you ways to ignite your health department. I want you to throw out everything you thought you knew about marketing and let's build your plan together!

Chapter 2 – Is Selling a Bad Word?

While attending an annual American Public Health Association APHA) Conference, I was struck by the sheer number of schools represented that teach some form of public health.

By volume alone, one would feel good about the future of public health. In attendance were over 12 thousand people, many of whom were students currently attending classes in the field.

This event gave me the time to visit each school's booth and question them about how they teach marketing to their students. Funny thing happened though; each school thought by the word "marketing" I was referring to the type of marketing that changes behaviors, such as smoking cessation or STD prevention.

When I explained that I was talking about the kind of marketing geared towards penetrating their community so that the public would be aware of the programs and services available at the local health department, most of them looked confused. Some even became defensive.

During a poster session, I visited with one presenter whose research showed exactly where fees and revenue came from related to her state's public health programs (such as immunizations, licenses, etc). While she enthusiastically deciphered her research for me, one of her colleagues listened intently to what we were discussing. When the researcher finished, her friend asked me why I was so interested in marketing public health? In her mind, it wasn't important whether or not her community was aware of the services her health department provides. She believed that the act of promoting those services was akin to drug companies trying to push pharmaceuticals on unsuspecting patients.

I shared with her the fact that I work with leaders of health departments across the country who are concerned about losing funding, are frustrated by the lack of public awareness of their services and are downright angry about lost opportunity to serve.

She shook her head and said, "We're public health, nobody cares 'til they need us."

That thinking is precisely what we are working to change!

Marketing your health department (selling public health) is not a bad thing, is it?

Have you ever been so excited about something that you just couldn't wait to tell people about it? Think back on this. Have you ever been involved with a group or organization that you just thought was fantastic? It's easy to sell something that you're passionate about.

If you had something that you really cared about, that you thought helped people. If you had a brand new program that could benefit somebody, aren't you doing them a disservice to not tell them about it? Selling is easy when you believe in what you have, and as an administrator of a health department, you have a myriad of services that you can sell, assuming that you believe in them.

Let's take WIC, for example. If you walked into a room full of low income, expectant mothers, wouldn't you want to tell all of them about WIC? Of course you would! Wouldn't you be willing to share with them all the benefits of WIC and how it can help them and their children? Again, it is very easy to sell something that you believe in.

On the other hand, if you're not passionate about the services that you have, you are probably not the right person for the job you currently hold. A lot of people think that "selling" is a bad word, but it's truly not. Selling is the act of sharing the good news with others. Selling is educating, it is the art of insuring your listeners understand what you have to offer, and because you are in public health and serving the needs of the public and of the community, you truly have multiple things to sell.

It's a great thing.

When I see our clients at conferences and they put their arms around me and tell me how much they care about what we've done for them, it makes me feel wonderful. It validates everything that I've worked for all these years. You, too, can have that same experience when you help people in your community.

Just because you do not own that health department and are a government employee doesn't mean that you don't have to have a personal connection with your customers. That's one of the myths and misconceptions that people have about people that work in health departments. They think because you don't own the health department, you really don't care about their needs. You're just a government employee, and you can keep your job whether you're successful or not.

This brings us back to the APHA conference. Those women that were concerned that they didn't have to sell their health department, that they have a ready built market, and a ready built customer base, are missing the boat completely. There is so much lost opportunity within your own county when you consider that one tenth of one percent of the community knows and can name ten of the things that you can offer them at your health department.

Let's get busy talking about selling, and exactly what selling is. Remember, selling is what happens once they get inside the health department. Selling is what happens when you're in a face-to-face, or on the phone with that client. Selling is the easy part and it's the fun part. If you don't find yourself talking quicker, your heart rate increasing, and a smile coming to your face as you try to explain the services that you have at your health department, we need to change your thinking.

If you discovered the cure for cancer, or the cure for baldness, wouldn't you want everybody to know about it? Wouldn't you stand on top of a building and scream at the top of your lungs, "I found it! I found it!" That's exactly how I want you to think about selling the services of your health department.

You are a salesperson, so embrace it

Most professionals have a hard time accepting that no matter what their education level or job description is, they are, indeed, in the sales business.

If you are employed in a tire shop, a restaurant, a health department or any other business that offers a product or service to a human being, you are in the sales business.

Now, there was a time when the term "sales" conjured-up an image of a door-to-door huckster selling pots and pans or snake oil. Many of the finest people I know are folks who have accepted their role as salespeople. From a pastor to a doctor and the volunteer, they know that any time you have to educate, inform or guide, they are, in fact, selling.

Selling isn't easy and it requires among other things, written goals. All sales professionals know how vital goal setting is to their success. They know it is necessary that our goals be written and succinct. We must start with the end in mind. Where do you want to be this time next week, next month and next year?

Writing them down isn't enough, the real secret is to share your goals with a close friend that will be your accountability partner.

A study from [2] Dominican University of California showed that people who wrote down their goals, shared with a friend, and sent weekly updates to that friend, were on average 33 percent more successful in accomplishing their stated goals than those who merely formulated goals. *(ref-2)*

_____

[2] *Ref 2*

Like the best salespeople in history, you now have one of the proven tools at the end of your pen, so start writing! It's as easy as closing your door and tuning into yourself and your dreams.

Chapter 3 – The Tower of Success

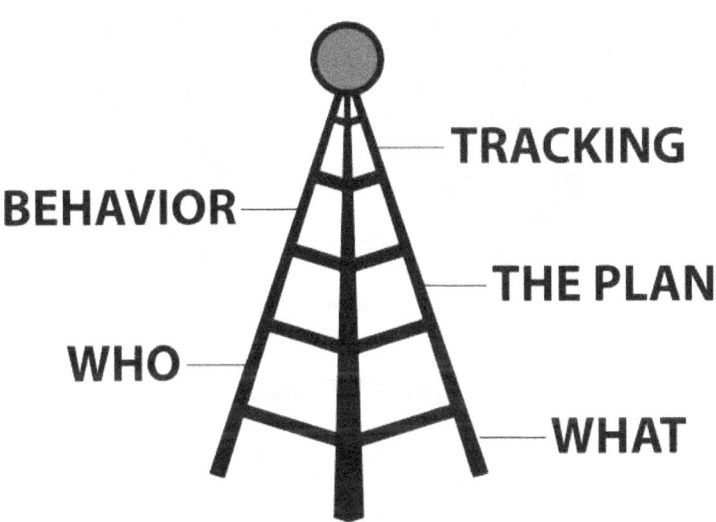

The tower of success consists of six different levels. Follow the program, go step-by-step, floor-by floor and you will have success, guaranteed. Skip a floor, or skip a level, and you're most likely going to fail. Just like a real building, you can't go from the first floor to the fifth floor, without going past the second, third, and fourth floors. By simply following these steps you will have success in selling public health.

Level one is what do we want to sell? It could be immunizations, it could be increased awareness of diabetes screening, it could be the new maternal health program that you have, it could be the dental program that you've had in place for years that nobody takes advantage of. We need to know what you want to sell, In order for you to pick what you want to sell, all you have to do is look around the health department and ask yourself, "What services am I struggling with? What programs do I see going away? What questions am I finding being asked by most of my customers?"

Another way to find out what you want to sell is to simply ask your staff and find out what programs they see the least amount of traffic in. Find out which services are not being utilized. This is a good place to start. You have to know what you want to sell in order to move to the next floor. I don't want you to get the wrong idea, you don't have to pick just one thing, you can pick multiple things. The bottom line is you need to pick something.

Take some time, look at the health department from an objective point of view, ask questions of your customers, look at what programs and services people don't know about, look at the things that you risk losing because of no traffic, and make a list of those things that you want to market.

It has to be compelling, it has to make your stomach burn, it has to be something that keeps you up at night. Only if you are completely, one hundred percent dedicated to expanding on that service, or making people aware of that service or program are you going to have any success whatsoever. It shouldn't be something that you take lightly. Remember, most decisions are made emotionally, not intellectually, and because of that you need to think from an emotional point of view at this time.

I know for a lot of people involved in public health that's a difficult thing to do. Logic rules; however today I want you to think emotionally. I want you to think about what's going to happen if you don't market that particular program? What's going to happen if people don't know about it? Make a list of what exactly you want to sell, what exactly you want to promote, and what things would make your health department more effective if people knew about them.

Level number two is Who is our audience? It's often been said that if you walk across a snowy field and look down at your feet, you're going to zigzag all over the place by the time you get to the other side. However, if you have a goal, if you have a fixed object on the other side of that field and you walk staring at that object, you will have a straight line when you look back at your footprints. The Who is that straight line!

We need to know who is the target market for that service. Let's say, for example, it is smoking cessation, then you need to know statistically who are most likely to be smokers? What age group or economic level is most likely to be a smoker? What education level is most likely to be a smoker?

Once you know who you are trying to sell, then we can create messages geared towards that "who", towards that market. Let's say for example it's bringing down the epidemic of obesity. Maybe your messages and your marketing needs to be geared towards people who are likely to not eat properly or exercise. Unfortunately, that's a large audience today, but let's say for conversation's sake that you're gearing this towards millennials. We need to create marketing geared towards that particular group. The first level, again, is what do we want to sell? The second level is, who is our audience, who do we want to sell to? Once we know those two things, we can now move to level three.

Level three is The Plan. You have to have a plan, just like the walking across that field in the snow, you have to know where you want to arrive. You have to have your expectations set. If you don't, you're just going to wander aimlessly through the process without any real success whatsoever. A plan is a step-by-step approach on exactly how you're going to sell those services to that particular group of people, to make them aware of those services, and to get them into the health department. The plan is something that can be changed as you move on through the process. The plan may start out as a paint by numbers approach with a focus on print media that will then turn into a focus on shoe leather outreach, but you have to start with a plan.

Now we know what we want to sell more of, we know who we want to sell it to, and now we're at level three where we need to do the plan. Once the plan is in place, you can move onto level four. Level four are the Actions or behaviors that you will take to achieve that plan. Once we know what behaviors we need to do, it's really just a matter of turning on the machine. It truly is that simple. Let's say, for example, that we know we want to sell more immunizations. We know that we've lost a lot of our market share to drugstore chains and grocery stores that are now providing flu vaccine and other immunizations. We know that we need to reach out and let people know that we are still here, that the health department provides immunizations for as little or less than the local grocery or drugstore chain. How do we get that message out?

One way is to create a direct-response-marketing campaign geared to a certain group of people. Once we know that we want to market to this group of people, we simply get together a mailing list and send compelling, outrageous marketing to that list informing them about our immunization program. That's one behavior.

Let's say we want to do effective marketing on our telephone system, so we create messages geared specifically during the time that we want to promote immunizations, where every message that people hear is about immunizations. While they're sitting on hold, we create a program where they hear about immunizations. When they call after hours, on weekends or holidays, they hear about your immunization clinic. You can also create a program where they hear about immunizations before the phone rings at the reception desk, which we call "Preemptive," or "Upfront" selling. Now we've done a mailing, we've done the marketing on our phone system, maybe the next behavior is we need to train the staff to inform every person that walks through the door about the immunization program.

Suppose we want to do an outreach and get out in the field, so we go to various community groups and civic organizations, do presentations about immunizations and why our health department gives immunizations. We reach out to sports teams and elementary schools. Once we start to establish these actions and behaviors, if we duplicate those behaviors and we commit to doing those actions on an ongoing basis, we will definitely have success.

The next level in the tower is tracking the results. It's nearly impossible to be successful at anything if you don't track the results of your efforts. It's often been said that the definition of insanity is doing the same things over and over that don't work, and expecting different results. One way to maximize your time, effort, and money is to track everything you do. Tracking is the simple act of creating methods that enable you to be certain whether or not a particular marketing approach is working. Take the phone messages for example. Many of our clients utilized call handling features that we've provided them, where we can actually track the number of callers that listen to the messages, the number of people that call after hours and the number of people that hang up. We can then compare those numbers with the amount of immunizations that are given during the period of time that we're doing the marketing. Now we can tell how effective that marketing is.

Example

Serving approximately 25,000 county residents, this small health department had only three employees.

The services they provide included breast and cervical cancer services, community education, community health services, environmental health, epidemiology, family planning, fluoride program, general health, HIV/AIDS testing and immunizations.

Just before the H1N1 crisis of 2009, the administrator and I had discussions about their needs.

Well aware that most people in her county had no idea of the services the health department provided, she wanted to promote those services more effectively. She was also concerned about her small staff being able to answer the telephone while they were holding a clinic.

We provided her health department with a program that automatically answered her telephone, marketed her services to every caller 24 hours per day (even when they were closed). Because she had a small staff, we further assisted her by adding preemptive messages that callers heard before the telephone rang at the receptionist's desk. This was used to answer frequently asked questions and free up the staff.

When the H1N1 outbreak occurred, we placed up-to-the-minute information on the "up-front" message so that panicked callers would be informed about when, where and how to obtain the vaccine.

Which often happens, this wonderful side benefit, freed her staff to administer vaccines and not be tied to the telephone answering the same questions over and over.

With tracking, we were able to prove the effectiveness of her marketing.

Fortunately, we know that this is very effective. When it comes to the mailing, there can be codes printed on the different mailing pieces so that we can determine whether or not those are bringing people into the health department for immunizations. This can be done with particular color codings or with numbers or letters. Tracking can also be done by simply having the patients carry in that card when they come to the health department for the immunization. It is very powerful to track each and every effort that you do, because when you track you will determine what's working, and what is not.

By the way, if you're familiar with the Pareto Principle of 80/20, you know that twenty percent of our efforts produce eighty percent of our success. By tracking which behaviors you are doing, and what they provide as an outcome, we can quickly determine which behaviors are not working, and which behaviors are working.[3]

Once we know this, we can focus on those twenty percent of behaviors that actually bring people into the health department, that increase the health departments good will and knowledge throughout the community.

The sixth and final level in the tower of success is Success. You have arrived when you are successfully marketing and bringing people into the health department. When you get people in the door as a result of your behaviors and marketing, then you have truly found the pathway to an evergreen solution that will ensure the health department has ongoing, duplicable campaigns that bring people in. The tower of success is not new, it's just a new way to think of a step-by-step approach to achieving the goals that you need in order to fix what's wrong with public health today. That biggest thing is nobody knows what you do.

_____

[3] *Ref 3*

Chapter 4 – The Paradigm - Social Media and Internet Marketing

In order to be effective at Internet marketing, you first must understand how fundamentally different search engines like Google and Yahoo are from social media sites such as Facebook.

As a search engine, Google users or businesses must understand how to develop methods to make their business surface first on Google during a search. To get a top ranking is all about thinking from the perspective of how an algorithm works as opposed to thinking how a human behaves. This is a problem.

With social media, for the first time, you can get a lot of traffic by creating something that people see and cannot resist sharing.

 So instead of thinking how you create something that will surface in the Google algorithm (which is essentially creating content for a robot), you're thinking, "How do I make something that inspires someone, that makes someone laugh, that makes someone feel better about their day or tells them something new that they will want to share with others?"

Going viral

Let's say you create a catchy video about smoking cessation and you link to it on your website. You draw 1,000 people to the video and they, in turn, share it with 500 more people. You now have 1,500 people that have viewed your content. Not a bad bump. Now let's say you share that video with 1,000 people and they share it with 2,000 and they share it with 2,000 more people and they share it with 8,000 and so on. It takes off and grows exponentially. This is the definition of "going viral."

A great way to generate interest in your social marketing is to create content that are fun lists, such as

13 ways to stop smoking, or the top 10 reasons to exercise.

In order for advertising of any kind to be successful, there must be an emotional resonance or humor to it that causes people to spread or share.

This is how substantive content will spread. Things spread through social channels now and that is how young people find things these days.

The world is changing more than ever now because we're all so connected. In the '70s and '80s, things like six degrees of separation and small worlds were intellectual curiosities. Now with the Internet, we are all actually connected with each other. For example with Facebook, you can use those six degrees of separation to spread your health department's message across the world.

When it comes to messages, it has been proven that social media is more likely to share and spread your content if it is fresh and even humorous instead of merely educational.

In their groundbreaking research, a group of students from [4]Brigham Young University set out prove that social media is more effective if it used in an entertaining way versus a purely educational way. Their research showed that an educational media

---

[4] *Ref 4*

campaign called "This is Public Health" reached 46,000 views in four years while the humorous video with a brief safety message entitled "Dumb Ways to Die" reached 11 million views in only four days! *(ref-4)*

They proved that without some entertainment value, there is less sharing and virtually no chance to achieve "viral status."

Chapter 5 – The Most Common Mistakes Health Departments Make

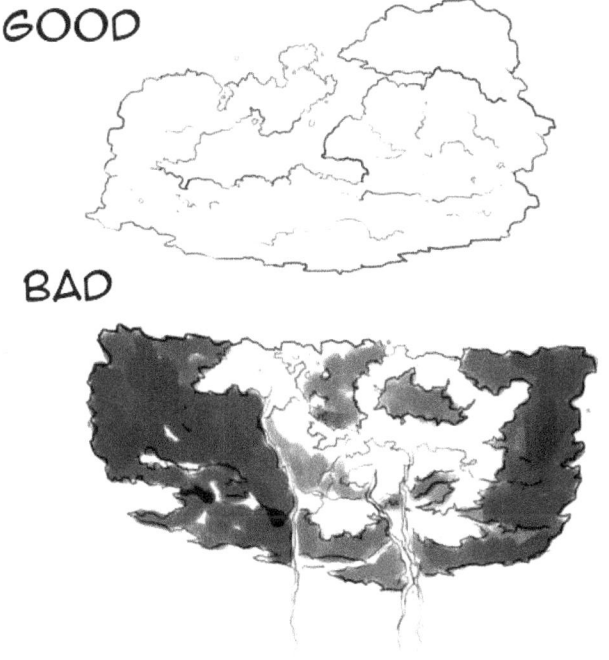

What are the seven most common mistakes with marketing that health departments make?

1) The person they put in charge of doing their marketing is not trained and has no idea how to do it.

2) They don't have systems installed or in place that will help them discover what works and what doesn't work.

3) The staff inside the health department have not been trained effectively on how to cross sell.

4) Ineffective outreach. It's more than sending out POs, PSAs, and ads in the newspaper. It means going out in the field.

5) Once somebody is in the health department, there's no system in place to funnel them into other life services.

6) Nobody knows what the difference is between marketing and selling. Marketing is the act of attracting people to even know who you are. Marketing is casting a wide net. It is the way that we go out and we try to get people to understand that there may be a need. It's uncovering those needs. It's looking under every stone. It's finding new creative ways to bring people's attention to you and who you are.

1. Selling, on the other hand, is once we get somebody in the door, the act of getting them to purchase or utilize your services. Selling is not a bad word. In fact, when there are systems in place, and behaviors that can be duplicated, selling can become quite enjoyable. In fact, it will also improve the morale at the health department. Again, "selling" should not have a negative connotation. Selling is following a

formula from A to B to Z. It is following a formula that works every single time. Once you learn the behaviors, you will know with effective tracking, that your behaviors lead to a positive outcome. You will then know that if you just simply follow these behaviors from a selling standpoint on a daily basis, you will be able to see quantum growth within the health department.

7) There is no paint-by-number system of attracting new clients to the health department. One way of doing that is by looking at your health department. We try to figure out exactly what your needs are, what's working and what's not working. A lot of times, new initiatives come along and new marketing ideas come along that are tried for a very short period of time. It's well known that most marketing or advertising takes months and months and months of repetitive action for anybody to even listen. There is so much noise out there. There's so much content, so much competition for the attention of the people that you want to get to your health department that you have to become a guerilla in marketing those services. In fact, there is a paint by numbers approach and once we discover what exactly you're doing that's not working, then we can create a paint by numbers approach where if you just follow the system, you will have outcomes on the other end that will be excellent.

The first step is the "business uncovery" and what does that look like. The business uncovery has different elements. Questions like, "How will you measure your success?" In other words, if you have no idea exactly what you're doing and what a successful outcome looks like, you're going to be lost. What is it that you want to happen? Sometimes it's as simple as just asking that question. What is it that you want to see? What are you trying to accomplish and what will you consider a happy ending? What's your destination? You're searching for the story that matters the most to your customer at the health department, the one you can deliver on all day, every day.

What is the message you deliver to a prospective client at the health department that distinguishes you from your competitors and makes the customer want to buy from you? What wonderful story is yours that hasn't been told? Don't try to tell the customer the whole story, just your best one. How long is the horizon? How long is it going to be before we figure if this is working? How much time do you have? When will the success be measured? Will you use advertising to promote your special event or limited time offer, or will you use advertising to become a household word? Targeting, do you prefer to attract reactional or transactional customers? Determine your ad budget, category dominance and so on. These are great ways for us to find out exactly what works, what doesn't work, what you need to do better and so on.

Chapter 6 – Lost Opportunity

What does lost opportunity cost and how can we stop it? Lost opportunity cost is something that is often staggering to people that we work with when they discover just how much opportunity there is right under their nose that they didn't even know about. In fact, I often ask them this question. If you found out that you were losing thousands and thousands of dollars worth of business a day, would you even want to know about it? If you knew about it, would you be willing to fix it? If you have a firm commitment to fix the problems that you have with the marketing of your health department, then, you will see quantum results.

Lost opportunity can be as simple as somebody who didn't know that you have diabetes screenings or a mother who comes in for maternal health and doesn't know that you have back to school immunizations for her older children. There's lost opportunity everywhere and once you categorize all of the services that you have, especially by which ones are being utilized, which ones are not being utilized and which ones you would like to see really expanded on, only then can you have this happen. Only then can you make quantum change that will end the lost opportunity. I look at lost opportunity cost as something that you have that you didn't even know about and it just takes small changes to turn that opportunity on often without any expense whatsoever.

What are the typical methods of marketing a health department? Many health departments truly follow the same pattern over and over. They do public service announcements. They get ads in the local paper. They print fliers that they hand out at the county fair or they may get a table. Some of them put ads in the local high school football program. Those are great things but they truly are not effective when it comes to attracting new customers. Why is that? The reason is that the community has been conditioned to ignore those ads and ignore the table at the fair because they see it all the time. The one way that you can definitely get attention is to be outrageous, is to interrupt their pattern. We often think of a pattern interruption as something as simple as saying a verb with a noun together. A verb before a noun, I mean, it sounds crazy but it actually works.

We worked with a health department that was trying to get more traffic to their family planning program because they've lost so much market share to the local doctors for family planning that the Public Information Officer (PIO) created an ad campaign that said, "Baby daddy no more." It was a brilliant idea for two reasons. One: it talked in the vernacular that most of the clients of her health department speak. In other words, the younger generation who speak like that. They would react and respond to that. Two: it gets across that unprotected sex will make you a "Baby daddy," so come on into the health department to learn about family planning services. The problem that she had was, there were old thinkers within her health department that shot that idea down. It was an out-of-the-box, brilliant idea that never saw the light of day. That would have been a major pattern interruption.

What are some creative ways to tap new markets? That is the secret sauce that we have. That is your secret sauce and only through questioning, only through a business uncovery, only through taking a deep, honest and often painful look at what you've done and what you have accomplished and what has not worked and what has worked can we find new markets and new ways to tap into your local community. I don't want to make this sound difficult because it truly is not. It's actually very simple.

In fact, it's a lot of fun when you start to think this way. If you just open your mind to all of the creative ways that your health department can help people within your community, it could be something as simple as telling people that are living in a higher income level than the typical customer of the health department that they should come into the health department for services. They do not need to be embarrassed to come in. It could be as simple as taking each and every customer that enters the health department and really sitting down and getting to know them and training your staff to look for opportunity and referrals. Referrals are a very powerful way to generate new traffic at the health department from the existing customer base. We'll talk about that later.

Chapter 7 – Partnerships

What are partnerships? Partnerships are a way that you can attract new business to the health department without a great outlay of cash. Partnerships simply mean you're going to partner with others that will benefit both of you. A lot of times, people within health departments are not aware that there are commercial ventures out there that would love nothing more than to simply have their name associated with something as great and healthy as the local health department. For example, we've spoken with several suppliers of goods to health departments from bandages and meds that would be willing to do co-oping. The more people that come into the health department to utilize services, the more demand it will create for their products. It will create more market share and more needs for their products that they sell within the health department. It's a win-win for everybody. Partnerships outside of the traditional partnerships in the community can be a great way without a lot of expense for you to attract new customers.

Chapter 8 – Direct Response Marketing

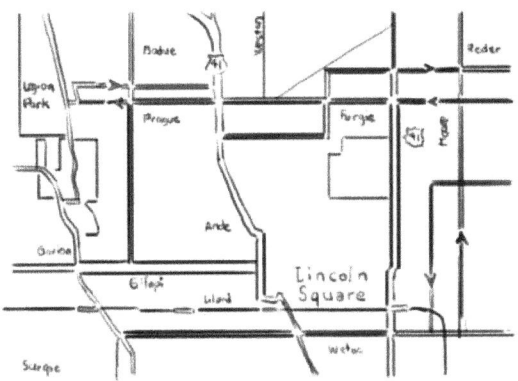

How does direct response marketing work? This is a big one. Imagine if you could reach out to people within any community, any neighborhood within your county or your health department district based on certain criteria. For example, let's say that your health department primarily serves people between the ages of 18 and 25 for STD treatment and testing. The other segment of your health department is the environmental health side, which really doesn't need any help because everybody has to have a license to run their business, their restaurant or get a septic permit, etc.

There are ways that you can target market specific neighborhoods and specific groups with marketing that is designed to create a pattern interrupt that is outrageous on purpose to really shake the trees. We specialize in helping our clients with that type of marketing. You have to have a major commitment and be willing to take the time to create with help, the direct marketing campaign and you have to have systems in place to track the major and minor changes that are required within your marketing to see what's working and what's not. Sometimes, it can take months and months of effort to discover the perfect postcard, the perfect letter, the perfect niche that you've never dreamed of. Once you discover that, it becomes truly evergreen. When I say evergreen, I mean it's a program or a marketing campaign that you can use forever that will bring essentially the same results that it did when it finally hit the home run.

Now, let's suppose that you have discovered one, two, three, four, maybe six different marketing campaigns that have created such a buzz that now you can turn those on at any time. You can take one of those marketing campaigns that you know now is evergreen and can run that marketing campaign for a period of time. Let's say for flu vaccine. You get through the flu season and move into the next season of the year where you know there are certain programs that traditionally have been used more. You can turn on that marketing campaign which you also know is evergreen, which you know produces results that you are certain to achieve, then you move onto the next season and start that campaign.

Direct response marketing is what I also call "outrageous advertising." It's outrageous because it says something, it attracts their attention in a way that they'd never dreamed possible. There are a lot of ways to do that, everything from outrageous packaging to outrageous headlines and so on. For example, we had one health department that sent out letters in a fake prescription bottle. Jammed inside the prescription bottle was the letter. Do you think that got opened and read? Absolutely!

Chapter 9 – Cross Selling

How can we cross sell in the office and over the phone? Cross selling is the act of taking somebody who is already a customer and getting them to buy other programs or utilize other services that they initially did not know about or had any interest in. I often use McDonalds as a perfect example of this. Have you ever been to the drive-thru at McDonalds and ordered a meal? What happens? The next thing you hear through the speaker is, "Would you like to super size that?" Or "Do you want an apple pie?" They know that when somebody becomes a customer, they're the easiest person in the world to cross sell or up sell. Your health department is really no different.

Now, cross selling takes a little bit of effort and it takes a commitment by you and your staff to ask every person that you come in contact with at your health department about their needs. Find out what their situation is. Most times, with just simple questioning and conversation, you will find that they have needs that you can meet with your other services or you may find that they have a relative that could use your services. Here's an example: Susie comes into the health department for a maternal health check up. In talking to Susie, the nurse finds out that her father is an invalid at home who needs help. That's an opportunity if you have home health to funnel Susie's dad into the home health program. It's that simple. Just by conversation and always looking for a way that we can increase and improve, are we going to be able to find those other opportunities for cross selling.

Another brilliant and very easy way to cross sell that every health department in the country should be doing is with their telephone system. What if you could put a message that plays before the call even gets to the receptionist? Let's say, for example, you've just started a new primary care program. When people call your health department, instead of just getting a ring-ring and the answer from the receptionist, now we have it announce, "Welcome to our health department. Be sure to sign up for our new primary care program, providing healthcare for your entire family when we pick up the line in the next three seconds." What do you think that would do? Do you think the 500 callers a month to your health department that all heard that up front before anything else would respond? Absolutely!

Cross selling can also be done in the office by using overhead audio. It can also be done with an on hold message program and even more powerfully, it can be done after hours with an after hours marketing program. Cross selling, remember, is just simple. It's taking one focus. Somebody comes in for item A and you tell them about the rest of the alphabet.

Chapter 10 – Inventive Marketing

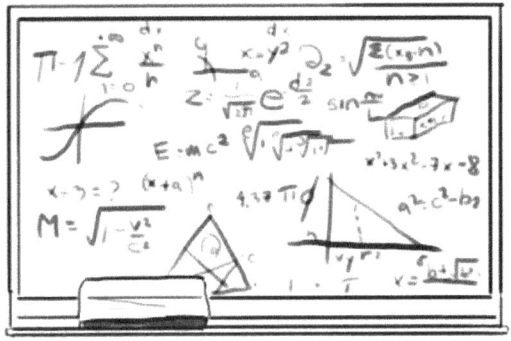

What does inventive marketing look like? This is the fun one. Inventive marketing is you utilizing that wonderful thing between your ears called your brain, which has wonderful creativity you may have never tapped into. Don't listen to Nay say or Sid say, "Oh, that won't work. This is the way we've always done it." Those are the type of people that never get anywhere. You have to be bold. You have to be outrageous and you have to trust your intuition and your instincts. If you're willing to do that and open up the creative flow within you and your team, you're going to see unbelievable results. Inventive marketing is, a means to get customers or patients to your health department. We have to find a way to throw a broad net to attract specific groups of people that currently do not know about the health department or its services. Inventive marketing is a paint by numbers approach that we're going to use to get these people in the door, to get them aware of who you are and to increase the respect that all public health departments deserve.

What are the daily behaviors one can do to turn things around? Daily behaviors are truly the road map to major success. You cannot control the outcome. You cannot control how many people are going to show up at your health department. You can't control how many people are going to need maternal health or immunizations or back to school physicals. You cannot control how many people are going to want to smoke or quit smoking. The one thing you can control is your behavior to attract those people to your health department. Daily behaviors are the end result of the work that we do with our clients once we discover what you need to accomplish. Then, you can create duplicative daily behaviors that will create more opportunity than you ever dreamed possible. A behavior is an action that you repeat on an ongoing basis because you know it's going to bring a certain outcome.

Now, here's an example: Let's say you are a salesperson outside of public health and your job is to sell insurance. You can sit in your office and wait for somebody to show up, which we call passive selling or you can get out and start attracting people to your office. You pick up the telephone and you start to call. Now, you don't know if you're going to actually talk to a person on the other end or get a busy signal. You don't know if that person's available but if you do behavior enough and start keeping track of what works and what doesn't work, you soon discover that if you pick up the phone and you make 25 dials, out of 25 dials, you're going to get to speak to five people. Out of those five people, four of them hung up or had no interest but one did. Now you know it takes 25 dials to get one person that you can speak to. Let's say you want to sell four a week. Then you need to do 100 dials to get four people that will listen to you.

It's just that simple. Once you know the behavior and you know the step-by-step approach of prospecting new clients, versus contact, versus interest, versus a body within your health department, versus a utilization of one-year services, you then have a daily behavior program that is like a well oiled machine. All you have to do is turn it on and it'll start pumping out opportunity.

Chapter 11 – What To Do with No Money

How to sell a public health department services when there's no money. This goes back to lost opportunity cost. We all know that budgets come and budgets go. The pendulum swings both ways. Some days there's so much money available, you don't know what to do with it and you only know you have to spend it before the end of the fiscal year or you won't get that same money next year. We also have experienced the opposite side where the pendulum, unfortunately, swings to the less fortunate end where budgets are cut, programs are eliminated and we start to see the morale and funding of the health department diminish. Unfortunately, that's where we are today with most health departments. Market share has been lost by competition from the local CVS store or local doctors, the Affordable Care Act, and more. That doesn't mean it's the end of the road. What it does mean is that you and your staff have now got to become experts at marketing, selling and start looking and seizing the moment, and opportunities that are there. There are opportunities everywhere.

How do you sell when there's no money? The first thing you do is you take a look at every person who comes into the health department. If you are not making sure that they know the entire menu of services that you have, if your staff have not questioned them or had a conversation designed to uncover possibilities and opportunities, you have completely missed the opportunity and missed the boat. It's just that simple. A lot of times a referral can bring more opportunity to you than you've ever dreamed. You'll never know unless you ask for the referral, unless you have a system in place to get that referral.

There are opportunities out there with partnerships that will cost you nothing. There are opportunities to market to callers on your telephone system that cost less than lunch for you per day that will provide immense opportunities. There is a way to do it. There is a method to attract business. There are methods that will attract business that will cost you virtually nothing. Don't let yourself be stymied or made incapacitated by the lack of funding.

We know that pendulum will swing back the other way eventually and once you create new profit centers or new methods that work, you will be completely immune the next time the pendulum swings the wrong way. The next time budgets are cut, you continue to do great business, you will continue to bring people in, you will continue to see your health department thrive and be a respected pillar in your community regardless of money. Wouldn't that be great? Wouldn't it be wonderful if you could create a health department that is immune to budget cuts where no matter what happens with funding from the state, or the federal government or your county board, you're still a vital effective resource in the community? It's true. It could happen.

Chapter 12 – Every Door Marketing

What is "every door marketing" and how does it work? Every door marketing is a way for you to again go for specific neighborhoods, specific streets to attract new business or opportunity from specific socioeconomic groups, even different education levels. This is not a bad thing. It's, in fact, a truly good thing. When you take the temperature and truly look at what you have as market share and where that market share is coming from, you can then discover what pieces of market you've never tapped into. You can find that there is a large segment of the population that you're not addressing, who have no clue who you are and how you can help them. This opportunity is truly there. It just takes that effort. Every door marketing is an ingenious way for you to reach out to specific streets, neighborhoods, groups, etc. without a great cost, with outrageous advertising or direct marketing concepts.

What are "done for you marketing" plans and how do they work? Sounds like fried chicken and gravy doesn't it? When you find an expert who can help you attract new business to the health department on an ongoing basis, wouldn't it make sense to just pay that expert to take care of that for you? It truly does. Done for you marketing is what we call the services that we provide for our clients. In other words, it can be as simple as a newsletter that goes out to everybody who has ever set foot in the health department, from the time we first meet them and on. It can be effective sales letters, it can be effective outreach, it can be effective partnership building. The point is, if you can find somebody that can provide these services for you in the health department, you will discover that you can focus on the things that matter most to you, which you probably have the background in: taking care of people.

Partnering with somebody who focuses on building your base is one of the easiest ways to turn the lights on at your health department. It's one of the most effective ways to make yourself immune from budget cuts. "Done for you marketing" is just finding that partner that will make it their mission to create, develop and track marketing campaigns to a point where they become truly evergreen, where we know they work and can turn them on and insert them at different times for different seasons for different programs and really get the business rolling.

Chapter 13– Call Handling

One of the most effective ways to attract and cross sell is by what we know as "call handling." Call handling is a way of managing your inbound calls so that they can be, A: up-sold, B: transferred through in the least offensive manner with the least amount of time, and C: can market even when the health department is closed. One of the biggest mistakes that every health department makes is how they answer their telephone. On one hand, they may have a receptionist who's sole job is to answer the telephone or it could be one of the staff members who, when they're not giving immunizations, is picking up the telephone. It could be an auto attendant, which is an automatic way that their phone system funnels calls. Both of those can work but they have to be handled professionally. Often times, the person who answers the phone is the least trained, least prepared person that could possibly answer your telephone and because their sole mission is to funnel the call, they've lost a lot of opportunity and they become jaded to answering the telephone.

Increasingly due to technology and budget cuts, more health departments are going to auto attendants. You know you have an auto attendant when you call a health department and it says, "Welcome to our health department. For immunizations, push 1, for epidemiology, press 2," and so on. One of the biggest problems with auto attendants is they were mapped out by either the phone technician or staff members who meant well but had no idea about call flow. This becomes painfully evident when you call a health department, and you hear 45 to 60 seconds of prompts. Push 3 for epidemiology, push 5 for WIC, etc. and you cannot get to anybody. What's happened? Well, they've achieved the goal of not having to pick up the telephone but what they've also done is dramatically lost market share and opportunity.

We know statistically that most people will hang up when they get a voice mail. We know statistically that most people will hang up and go away when they get an auto attendant. Why in the world would you want an auto attendant that doesn't serve the caller, that drives them away and loses that opportunity? You don't. If you have to have an auto attendant, you want one that is friendly, very quick and engages them. That cannot be accomplished by having the technician's voice on the phone system or the receptionist that you fired two years ago who's voice is still directing calls. You need to select and partner with somebody who can help you set those up and track the time it takes to get through to somebody, the time it takes to get the information that the average caller wants. Often times, we find that there's been no research done whatsoever within that health department to determine who most people that call the health department are trying to reach.

Let's say, for example, it's your WIC clinic. Why in the world would you make WIC number 7 or 8 in those prompts instead of number 1? It could be that the health department is getting calls for environmental health when, in fact, environmental health is a different phone number. We've actually heard auto attendants with people that we've helped that started out with, "Thanks for calling our health department, if this is for environmental health, hang up and dial 555-555-1212, please listen carefully because our menu items have changed," blah, blah, blah. What happens is the average caller is hanging up. They don't want to hear that. There are other ways to handle that call that will eliminate that problem. It can be as simple as creating a direct dial button where instead of having people dial the actual number to environmental health, they can press a key that can be programmed in your phone system that will direct them there immediately without having to waste their time listening to 15 seconds worth of telephone numbers.

Call handling is maximizing every single opportunity with a caller and making sure that their arrival there on your phone system is enjoyable, quick and efficient. Call handling is the ability to sell and market your health department, create an image that will drive people to your health department that will change the way people see your health department. Call handling enables you to get the message out after hours. It enables you to get the message out before they talk to a staff member. It enables you to get the message out when they're sitting on hold. Call handling is truly one of the most remarkable and cost effective ways to improve the image, the market share, and the morale of your health department with almost no expense.

Chapter 14 – Accountability & Coaching

Why is coaching and ongoing training so valuable and important? Having been involved in business my entire life, I can tell you that I have personally trained thousands of people how to sell and how to market. One thing I discovered a long time ago was that in a meeting, I could train people to do a specific behavior, get them motivated and get the Ra-Ra-Ra session going. It could be a two-day meeting. They'd walk out the door and they would be inspired and ready to go. The great David Sandler once wrote, "You can't teach a kid how to ride a bicycle at a seminar," and that's true. You can go to seminar after seminar within your local health association on how to improve various things and while you walk out feeling good, after a while, the impact wears off. (ref-5)

Why does that happen? It happens because other things occur in your daily activities and in your life and in your business that it becomes less and less important and less and less on the tip of your tongue and before you know it, all the things that you've learned at that particular conference or meeting that you were so inspired by are completely gone. Usually, it seems to last a week or so. If you don't believe me, just ask yourself when was the last time you got involved in a weight training campaign or a health diet for yourself? Most people don't make it past two weeks.

Ongoing coaching and ongoing training is valuable and important because it ensures that you are going to see the benefit of what you want, and what you want to achieve. Ongoing training is so vital because it gives you accountability. That's something that's truly lacking. Most of the people that I personally work with have nobody they can truly talk to within their health department about the problems they're having. Most of the administrators that I help can't go to the girl that answers the phone and share with her the worries that she may have about how we're going to be able to pay for the rest of our staff the rest of this year because the funding's been cut. Having a coach is having a third party non-emotional participant who can help you see through the fog of emotion.

It's been said that in adult training, it takes a minimum of 600 hours to internalize even one concept. They say that it takes about 10,000 hours to become an expert in anything. Well, I'm here to say that I'm an expert in teaching people how to sell and market their health departments. I have helped numerous administrators that have become experts in the same thing. What did it take? It took a commitment on their part and ongoing coaching. What happened was they discovered that the concepts that they heard initially from our training didn't really have an impact on them until maybe a year or two down the road of ongoing coaching. After they'd heard the same concept five or six times, finally a light bulb went off and they said, "Oh, I get it. Now I understand. Now I'm ready to do this."

What happens is now that they are armed with that knowledge, have internalized those concepts, and now that they have begun to see the benefits of having a third party non-emotional coach who they can turn to and discuss what works, what doesn't work, what they need to change to help them debrief each and every new program they try to initiate, only then, can they really see the true benefits of this type of marketing. Whether you plan on working with us or somebody else, I highly recommend that you seek out a coach that can offer you ongoing coaching and training that will help you get to where you want to be. It's the same thing for professional football, basketball, baseball and any professional sport. The athlete is great but they become truly tremendous and unbelievable when they hire a coach to take them to the next level.

In the 2016 Summer Olympics in Rio, Michael Phelps became the most decorated Olympic athlete of all time. Although he had won gold many times before, he only achieved this level of greatness with the help of his coach.

Everybody needs a coach for something.

Chapter 15 – Four Ways to Grow a Successful Health Department

You've spent years learning your field. You have more professional and academic certifications than you did last year, but there is one thing you may have overlooked.

That one thing is how to build a sustainable health department with annual growth instead of agonizing entropy.

There are four areas of development we will focus on in this series:

1) Getting Customers

2) Keeping Customers

3) Growing Customers

4) Expanding Customers

First, lets focus on getting customers, which requires marketing, selling and otherwise acquiring the herd.

First, you must identify your market. Are you seeking certain income levels or age groups? Are you reaching young adults with messages targeted at their interests, needs and fears?

Do you know where they are and have you created viable "entry points" to funnel them in?

Many times we see and hear messages that fall on deaf ears. Does your message content resonate with your audience?

In order to move people to action, you need to tap into the emotional factors that drive them. For many that arrive at your health department, that factor is pain or fear.

While we don't wish pain or fear upon anyone, the good news is that these are the absolute strongest decision-making emotions.

It has been said many times that people make decisions two ways, either intellectually or emotionally. As one involved in the health and well-being of your customers, you are at a major advantage when the marketing battle commences.

Now, you just need to craft a consistent and compelling message and focus on the next step, which is Keeping Customers. You have served them, now you must nurture the relationship by creating an experience that will create retention.

Let's start with designing the experience. When customers walk into your health department, what do they see? How are they greeted? How are the telephones answered? What do they hear when their call is placed on hold?

Have you made a conscious decision on how to make each step of your process enjoyable? From every contact with the staff to each telephone call and email, there must be a concentrated effort to make the experience the best it can be.

Another key to keeping customers is conditioning them to behave a certain way. This can be as simple as recognizing possible future opportunities to serve them. Take the expectant mother, for example. What possible future services can you make her aware of? Will she need child health, immunizations or WIC?

Now that you have identified possible future opportunities, how are you going to develop a relationship that will keep you in the forefront of her mind? Do you have a monthly newsletter campaign? I often coach clients on how vital a newsletter can be to building an ongoing relationship with their community.

Orchestrating the experience means that every contact, email or conversation is planned to create a win-win for the customer and your health department.

Surveys have proven time and time again that most customers cease doing business with you because they feel taken for granted. Do the people you serve feel like they are talking to a bureaucratic agency or do they experience a nurturing relationship based on mutual respect?

Next we focus on the next step, which is Growing Customers. You have served them. You have nurtured the relationship by creating an experience that will create retention, now let's talk about increasing the value of what you do by creating next steps in the process.

Do you have an ascension program? When you look at your health department and the list of programs and services you provide, you may notice that some of those items can be cross-sold to customers. For example, the young couple who are in for family planning. Is it possible they will need prenatal care or WIC some day?

How about the gentleman who came in seeking a septic permit? Is it possible he might need home health, immunizations or a free health screening?

The idea of this step in the process is to understand that each interaction you have with a customer or patient need not be the one and only. In fact, once you realize this concept, you will see your numbers soar!

<u>What should happen first / next?</u>

Take a look at each visitor in the last 30 days and place them into categories, such as those seeking medical or health services, mothers, elderly and those seeking non-health related services, such as vital statistics, permits and inspections.

Once you have completed your review, ask yourself what additional services might each person in these categories need next?

Now it is time to move on to the fun part, which is reaching out to these people.

The next step is Expanding Customers.

Did you know that referrals are one of the most effective methods of increasing awareness and use of your programs and services? It's true!

People that utilize your services are likely to have friends, family members and acquaintances that are in the same place they are (socially, economically and health-wise). Therefore, would it not make sense to ask them for referrals?

Environmental health is often seen as the enforcer instead of the good guys who keep restaurant food safe, water clean and other hazards at bay. Why not partner with those seen by staff from food handler's classes to promote healthy food choices?

Another powerful and under appreciated opportunity lies in joint ventures. Try partnering with businesses that promote a healthy lifestyle, such as bicycle shops, gyms, yoga and martial arts?

They want their message heard too, why not share the cost of buying media time?

Chapter 16 – Five Ways to Improve your Health Department, Even During a Budget Crunch!

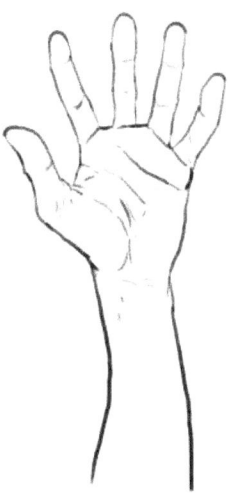

In times like these, some fall like old trees and some reach new heights they never thought possible.

Has this happened to you? You're at a conference and you see the same faces from around your state. Some never seem to grow and some are going gangbusters?

What do they have that you don't have? How can they be so successful even during budget cuts? They have figured out that while most people wither in the face of adversity, they have seen great opportunity in the holes created by budget cuts.

Here are five easy (and affordable) ways to turn your health department into a sizzling success!

1. <u>24/7 Marketing</u> – [5]Research shows that callers prefer to listen to pre-recorded information about their health department's programs and services versus asking staff. Most are embarrassed by the fact that they are in need. A 24/7 marketing plan allows you to set up a hotline that they can call into at their leisure and listen.

   A good 24/7 marketing program will let you track the number of calls and the number of people who listened to the message and who hung up.

2. <u>Messages On Hold</u> – It has been proven time and time again that the single most effective advertising is done right on your telephone. According to a [6]poll by CNN, 70% of callers made a purchase based on an offer they heard

---

[5] *Ref 5*

[6] *Ref 6*

from an on-hold message. Your telephone system should be looked at like your own TV station. You have a captive audience. *(ref-6)*

3. <u>Up-Front Marketing</u> – If you could wave a magic wand and tell everyone in your community about one program or service your health department has, what would that be? Up-front marketing allows you to play an up-front message to every caller to your health department before the call is sent through. Even if you only receive 20 calls per day, that's 400 people a month that would be made aware of your information. Powerful!

4. <u>Voicemail Radio</u> – Imagine if you could direct callers to a monthly radio show about your health department right on your own telephone system? What about during flu season when it could announce updated clinic dates each week?

5. <u>Web Audio</u> – Does your website talk to visitors? This is an excellent way to drive more visits to your website or Facebook page.

Chapter 17 – Consider It Done!

Recently, I attended a conference at an Orlando resort. On the telephone in my room was a button called "Consider It Done," which I found amusing.

Unable to resist the urge, I pressed the button and promptly got a nice staff member on the line who answered, "Consider it done, how can I help you?"

When I asked what "Consider it Done" meant to her, she said that their hotel believed in service so whole-heartedly that this was their mantra. She shared with me that they spend millions of dollars each year on marketing and advertising, and with that kind of investment, they don't want to drop the ball.

This got me thinking about how wonderful it was to find a company so dedicated to their ongoing success that they went to the trouble of putting "Consider it Done" buttons on their telephones.

When you look at your health department, do you see a confused message? Do the people in your community know what services you provide or not?

If you're like most health departments, you probably have thought about making the community aware of your services but have put it on the back burner to be done later. You may have started a marketing campaign but it fizzled due to lack of focus.

I speak with many directors and administrators of public health departments across the nation weekly. Some are focused on solving the age-old problem of public ignorance regarding their services and programs while others are procrastinators.

Are you ready to invest the time, money and energy to make your health department a center of the community, recognized for high quality care, or are you comfortable with the status quo?

Like the hotel in Orlando, are you ready to maximize the success of your health department with a "Consider it Done" button of your own, or are you satisfied with diminished funding, mistaken public perception and confusion?

If you are ready to "Consider it Done," open up your mind to the many affordable ways you can market your health department, such as on-hold marketing, voicemail radio and lobby marketing, just to name a few.

Chapter 18 – Holes in Your Bucket?

D o you have a system for attracting referrals? It has been said that a referral from a happy customer costs many times less than acquiring a new customer by any other means. If this is true, why don't all businesses have a system to gain referrals?

You just didn't know how

Many years ago, my mentor and business coach taught me a system for gaining (and giving) referrals that truly works. Professionally targeting referrals leaves the guesswork out of the equation while protecting your "referrer's" reputation. It all comes down to communication. Most people love to help others, it makes them feel good and validates their decision for doing business with you.

Some tips

Set a meeting with your referrer to convey your expectations. This is your opportunity to discuss not only what you want your referrer to say, but also how you will report back at each step of the sales process with their referrals.

It is not just the name

Most people think that giving a name is a referral. We define a referral as a person who knows your name, your company and is expecting your call. It's a higher standard, yes, but you are worth it.

Chapter 19 – In The News

Recently the news is full of stories about the reappearance of whooping cough, the Texas West Nile outbreak, the Hantavirus in Yellowstone Park and even bubonic plague. While these have broken though the myriad of media, they underscore the need for the CDC and local health departments.

Just like Hurricane Katrina illustrated the need for good leadership at FEMA and 911 taught us how important it was that the FBI share information with the CIA and local law enforcement, the news is full of good reasons why the local health department is important and necessary!

As we wait for the election season to end and the other shoe to drop regarding funding, cases like these ensure that public health will see the light of day.

They don't think of us till they need us!

Chapter 20 – The Power of a Shock and Awe Marketing Campaign

I GET IT!

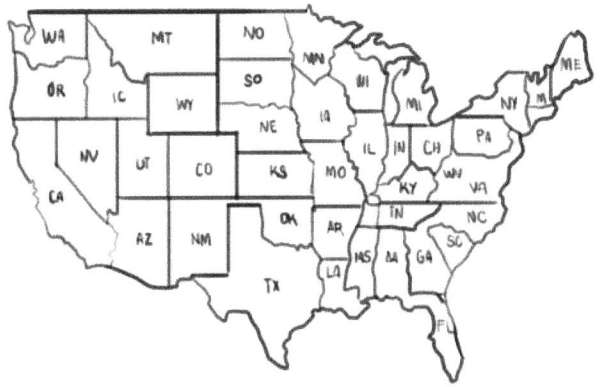

As you sit and contemplate your next move to market your health department, you are probably feeling a little lightheaded from all the questions you have. How are you going to break through all the noise that your target market hears every day? Who cares what the health department has to offer? How can we afford to make things happen with shrinking budgets?

One method of gaining the attention of your community is a tactic we call "shock and awe."

This is an all out planned barrage of focused marketing so different, so overwhelming it breaks through.

Several years ago when the new public health logo was unveiled, I must admit I was excited and hopeful that we might be seeing the development of a brand. While it was a milestone, it seems to have become nothing more than a logo.

As I mentioned, there are so many affordable methods available to every health department, one could easily do a "shock and awe" campaign that could be sustained and would bear fruit.

Some methods we use to help public health departments include sales letters, press releases, outrageous ads, on hold marketing, voicemail radio and training on how to create a buzz that breaks through the noise.

However you do it, a shock and awe campaign will certainly bring results. Remember, in marketing, different is always better.

Chapter 21 - Shoe Leather Outreach

Since the beginning of public health in England with the cholera outbreak in the 1800s, door-to-door outreach has been one of the most effective means of educating the public. In his ninth year as Virginia's Chesterfield Health District Director, Dr. Parham Jaberi is on to something.

An idea

Starting his career in Louisiana Public Health, Dr. Jaberi was faced with a syphilis outbreak in a small neighborhood. He set up two public health nurses to do STD and HIV testing at the local community center while staff went door-to-door. Neighborhood residents were informed that there was free STD testing going on and while there, staff were able to educate residents about the services the health department provides. "We did see a slight up-tick in services in a community that hadn't used them before."

Today a process

Noticing a 10 to 15% decrease in family planning and WIC clientele, he decided to try what he calls, "Shoe-leather Epidemiology." On the eve of the 2015 hurricane season, he and his staff began an emergency preparedness exercise knocking on 472 doors to provide information on emergency preparedness, including what items are needed in their EP kit. While there, they spoke about women's health and WIC. They also took the opportunity to drop off a tri-fold brochure listing the programs and services available at the health department for the community.

Of the 112 people that answered the door, 80 engaged in meaningful conversation.

"Being a relatively conservative area, I was concerned that people might view this negatively as big government, but got the opposite response where people were actually appreciative that they were being taken care of. We got a lot of positive feedback that day," said Dr. Jaberi.

Lost opportunity

One of the things we help our public health clients with is recognizing lost opportunities to market their services. This exercise uncovered a segment of the community largely unaware of the health department. "Most of our services are used by the young and pregnant moms; many senior citizens said this was the first time someone from public health had come in contact with them."

Added benefit

People can spend years working in the same health department without crossing paths. This can lead to misunderstanding, lack of communication and lost opportunity. Dr. Jaberi shared, "This brought staff, who normally don't work together on a day-to-day basis out of their silos. I saw what a morale booster it was for my team."

In speaking with Dr. Jaberi, I was struck at the creativity he used in impacting his community. While some may think going door-to-door is akin to being a vacuum cleaner salesman, he and his staff proved that nothing beats face-to-face contact. Although they did not have a tracking mechanism in place to look for increased traffic at the health department, the success of the outreach is unquestionable.

Why not do the same thing at your health department? What would happen if you spent one Saturday per quarter going door-to-door? Would you see an increase in awareness of your services? Would you see a boost in morale?

Shoe leather outreach works!

Chapter 22 – The Power of Money (and why the tobacco campaign has been successful)

That headline is a little misleading in that it depicts money as the driving force for the recent tobacco prevention successes. While money plays a necessary role in getting the message out, it's only one piece of the puzzle.

In his book [7]"The Wizard of Ads," Roy A Williams explains that it's not about reaching too many people, it's about repetition. "The average radio ad needs to be heard by the same listener at least 3 times within 7 nights sleep, week after week after week. Don't skip weeks. Sleep erases advertising."

As true as that statement is, we know it takes a huge budget to pay for that repetition. Unfortunately, most health departments do not have that kind of money to invest in marketing. *(ref-7)*

What do you do?

The only way to reduce an ad's need for repetition is to craft a message of such credible urgency that a significant number of listeners will take action even though they are not yet in the market for the product in question.

Let's face it, most people only think of their health department as the place you go for STD testing. How do you get their attention for immunizations, free screenings and family planning?

Unless you've been under a rock, it's hard to miss the barrage of anti-tobacco ads. From billboards to television and radio, the campaign has been very successful.

---

[7] *Ref 7*

Sure, it costs a lot of money to create ads and get them in the eyes and ears of the public on such a wide scale, but how do you do something for your local health department? You take full advantage of every resource you have at your disposal.

1. Newsletters - Do you have a monthly newsletter that reaches out to your customers, stake holders and the general public? It's easy and low cost.

2. On hold marketing - Do you have a program to market your services to callers while they sit on hold? This is the most direct form of targeted advertising, yet it is the most powerful. A captive audience!

3. Lobby promotions – What do people hear while they sit in your lobby or waiting room? An in-store audio marketing program is not just for banks and huge retail stores. They are affordable and as easy to set up as the on hold marketing program.

4. Seminars and webinars - What groups do you give free talks to each month? From the local chamber of commerce to church groups, Rotary and even school assemblies, there are free opportunities everywhere.

5. Press releases and op-ed pieces - These free tools offer opportunities to reach your public and market your services. The local paper is

hungry for content and it creates a win-win situation.

6. Cooping - Who do you buy supplies from? Who wants to reach the same demographic that you do? Find these companies and have them cover the cost of your next big campaign. This is a virtual treasure chest of funding that is out there to be harvested. Yet most health departments are unaware of the potential.

7. Twitter, Facebook and other social media – It's not just for kids. Social media doesn't rely on an algorithm like Google to be successful; it relies on people sharing content that moves them. With social media, for the first time, you can generate a lot of traffic by creating something that people see and cannot resist sharing.

Instead of trying to create something that will surface in the Google algorithm, which is essentially creating content for a robot, you should make something that inspires someone, that makes someone laugh, feel better about their day or tell something new that they will want to share with others.

You may not have the budget and resources the CDC has, but you can do much better with the resources you do have. The question is, will you?

Chapter 23 - The Virus of Positive

Today the term "going viral" paints a clear picture of YouTube phenomena like a kid jumping a bike off the roof of his house or cute kittens drawing millions of views. What we're really talking about here is the time-tested wonder called word of mouth.

Back in 1890, Chicago was picked to host the next World's Fair. Excitement grew as fast as the anxiety of knowing that this event had to be so spectacular as to dwarf the most recent World's Fair in Paris (where the Eiffel Tower was introduced).

In order to create a world-class experience, the finest architects, engineers and visionaries from the United States were selected. Among them was site designer and landscaper Fredrick Law Olmstead, the man who designed New York's Central Park.

Olmstead knew the power of creating a positive experience and how it would cause people to share their thoughts with family and friends. He knew what viral marketing was before the turn of the century!

"It was critical now,"[8] Olmsted argued, "to concentrate on making improvements of a kind most likely to increase the gleam in the stories people took back to their hometowns." *(ref-8)*

"This is the advertising now most important to be developed; that of high-strung, contagious enthusiasm, growing from actual excellence: the question being not whether people shall be satisfied, but how much they shall be carried away with admiration, and infect others by their unexpected enjoyment of what they found."

Are your customers carried away with admiration and unexpected enjoyment in what they've found? There is power in positive!

---

[8] *Ref 8*

Chapter 24 – What's Funny About Environmental Health?

"Here they come, those pesky people from the health department trying to shut down that restaurant." "What happened to your septic tank?" "The health department came by and gave me a ticket."

Cops!

Does the public look at you like a predator or do they see you as the good guys? Maybe it's time for an image makeover for environmental health?

When asked, most people think only about two things a health department does:

1. Sexually Transmitted Diseases
2. They shut down restaurants, don't they?

One of the most effective ways to create an impression is to take the one the public has of you (right or wrong), and use that as a starting point.

What do I mean?

Why not use humor about environmental health and through laughter, educate the public about how good you are? You're probably thinking, "How can anything about environmental health be humorous?"

History is full of public health heroes.

From Florence Nightingale and Louis Pasteur to Jonas Salk and Walter Reed, we all have benefited from the behind the scenes work of people just like you.

From the 1850s when Dr. John Snow directed that pump handles be removed from wells so citizens had to go elsewhere for water (which ended the cholera epidemic), to the tireless efforts of your own environmental staff, some are forced to take a paternal role in society.

Not too long ago, restaurants, airplanes and even hospitals were full of cigarette smoke. Thankfully, that is a thing of the past.

One director recently sent me the following regarding changing public perception about her Environmental Health Division:

"EH is tough to market in that we are regulatory and not a "money maker" for the Health Department. We are also a silent arm in the sense that if we do our jobs, no one really knows what we do because you do not see the effects of our work - you simply get what you expect and no one gets sick."

Why not take the wonderful work of that "silent arm" and bring it to the forefront of your marketing campaign?

If Progressive and Geico can sell insurance using humor, so can you. For more information on how, contact us.

Chapter 25 – Why Public Surveys Work

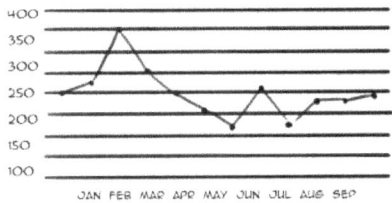

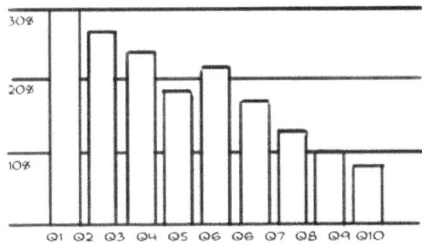

In order for a doctor to find out what issues a patient has, she must first ask about the symptoms. Only after effective questioning can the doctor prescribe the correct treatment to get the patient healthy again.

One of the most effective ways to jumpstart your marketing begins with taking the temperature of your market.

In other words, you need to uncover what it is they like (and don't like), about your health department.

A community outreach survey can provide valuable information to help guide you on the correct strategies to understand your particular community and therefore maximize your marketing efforts.

Getting your community involved can help create a sense of goodwill while helping you understand where you may be lacking in services offered.

To start, simply write down a list of questions formulated to help you understand the symptoms of your market. These questions can be multiple choice and brief enough to be easily answered online, via email, in your lobby or on handouts.

Some examples include:

1. Have you ever used the services of our health department?

2. How likely are you to use our services in the next year?

3. Are the office hours 9-5 Monday through Friday convenient for you?

4. Which of our services would you like to obtain from our health department?

5. What can we do to better serve you and your family?

6. What services would you like to see added?

7. Would you be willing to pay a per-visit fee? If so, how much?

Asking questions will help you develop a laser-like focus on how to effectively market you health department. Now, where did you say it hurts?

Chapter 26 – How Memorable Is Your Message?

Can you complete this sentence? "Winston tastes good like a ..."

If you were born before 1965, you probably had no trouble reciting the tag line from the ubiquitous Winston Cigarette commercial.

There has not been a cigarette commercial on television since January 1, 1971!

Why, then, do we remember such an insignificant jingle?

Repetition!

Many of the clients I have helped arrived with the mistaken assumption that their message should deliver immediate and awesome results. They have been disappointed, frustrated and downright angry that the magic bullet they fired did not create a stampede towards their door.

Broca and it's secret.

In his groundbreaking book "The Wizard of Ads," Roy H. Williams tells us about the magic keys to unlocking the subconscious part of the mind, broca. He goes on to illustrate how this gatekeeper needs to be "tricked" to lower his guard enough to allow our message to resonate with the subconscious to become part of our conscious awareness.

One of the keys to broca is undying repetition mixed with unpredictability. This is why most of the clients I coach understand that it takes approximately 600 hours for an adult to "own" a new concept.

Your message is no different. Your audience, be they on the phone, in your business or driving down the road, need to be stimulated by your content repeatedly.

Your message is no different.

Instead of doing what everyone else does, try being unconventional with messages that call people to action.

Remember, persuasion is not a new kind of shoe leather.

Chapter 27 – Crazy But It Works Like Magic!

Each New Year, everyone talks about resolutions and goals. This happens annually yet most don't achieve more than a couple goals, if any at all.

Back in the 80s, a young fellow by the name of Tony Robbins became a household word in the self-help industry with his book "Unlimited Power" and the life coaching industry that followed.

While some of Robbins' methods seemed unusual (fire-walking), he was sought out by CEOs, NFL teams, politicians and even the military to teach what successful thinking can do.

After years of infomercials, I decided to buy his tape series to listen to while on weekly business trips. The package included a workbook with assignments that you completed as you went through 30 days worth of tapes.

One such assignment was goal setting. I had read about the importance of goal setting in books authored by his predecessors, yet I had never taken it seriously and written out my goals.

Alone in a hotel room, what else is there to do?

Robbins asked that we open up the workbook to the two blank pages and as we listen to some soothing music for 30 minutes, write down EVERYTHING we want to be, accomplish, own, attain, change, etc. It didn't matter how ridiculous it may seem, you were to write it down and I did. If you wanted to learn to speak a foreign language, fly an airplane, build a business, you wrote it down.

After the goal exercise, we were instructed to close that page and look at it a year later. As time went on, I forgot the goal setting workshop. In fact, about 18 months went by before one night I happened upon the workbook and started glancing through it. When I got to the section on goal setting I was shocked so much that I actually yelled out loud!

Out of the goals I had set almost two years ago, most had actually been achieved! Without going into personal details, I can share with you that astounding things had occurred that when I originally wrote them out, seemed crazy, unbelievable and would never happen.

One of the over 50 goals I wrote that night was to work with a very famous person we all know (we will call him Mr. X). This was an impossible thing to happen because after all, we were in two different parts of the world and had no reason for our paths to cross.

Over the past nine years, Mr. X and I have worked on many projects together and have become personal friends.

Since that night when I looked at my forgotten list, I make an annual, free form list of goals around the first of the year. Whatever pops in my head, no matter how big, small, important or silly, I write them down. I don't look at the list until the end of the year.

I invite you to do the same this year. It is crazy, it is magical and it works!

Chapter 28 – Going Viral

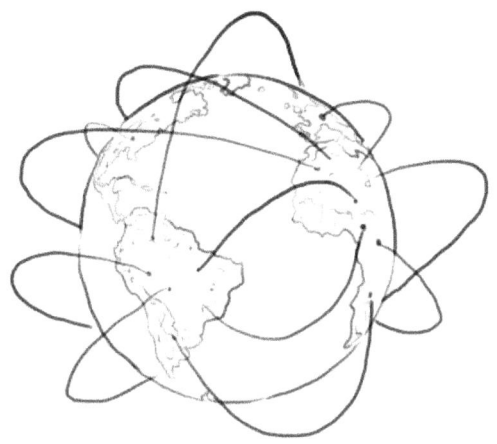

What is the definition of going viral? Let's say you create a catchy video about smoking cessation and you link to it on your website. You draw 1,000 people to the video and they in turn share it with 500 more people. You now have 1,500 people that have viewed your content, not a bad bump.

Now let's say you share that video with 1,000 people and they share it with 2,000 and they share it with

2,000 more people and they share it with 8,000 and so on. Now it takes off and grows exponentially.

A great way to generate interest in your social marketing is to create content that are fun lists such as 13 ways to stop smoking or the top 10 reasons to exercise.

In order for advertising of any kind to be successful there must be an emotional resonance to it (or humor) that causes people to spread or share.

This is how substantive content will spread. Things spread through social channels now and that is how young people find things these days.

The world is changing more than you can imagine because we are all so connected. In the '70s and '80s, things like six degrees of separation and small worlds were intellectual curiosities. Now with the Internet we are all actually connected with each other. Now with Facebook, you can use those six degrees of separation to spread your health department's message across the world.

Chapter 29 – Why Your Customers Feel Uncomfortable

We all do it. We don't mean to, but on some unconscious level we all put off our customers by "talking shop."

Let's face it; everyone wants to feel important and relevant. Nobody likes to feel dumb or uninformed, but did you know that by using certain words or "talking shop" in front of your customer, you are making them feel uncomfortable?

In the book "I'm OK-You're OK," Dr. Thomas Harris introduced us to the groundbreaking concept of Parent-

Adult-Child or (PAC) in Transactional Analysis or (TA) *(if you are unfamiliar with the last two sentences, you may be feeling uncomfortable right now).*

How does this affect your business?

In every conversation, you and the other person each take on one of the three states. The ideal being Adult to Adult. The worst is Parent to Child, but why?

Let's take an example of a waiter in a restaurant who gets confused and brings the wrong order to your table. You can respond with understanding and courtesy, "That's ok, we get to enjoy our conversation longer," or you can snap at the waiter, "This is terrible service, why can't you get it right?"

In the latter example, you were the angry Parent, which by default puts the waiter in the Child state (nobody likes to be here, to feel dumb, to look bad).

Big words make small success

Whether it's in public health, medicine, an auto parts store or lawn maintenance, every business has words or technology that are only understood by those that are trained in that field. Yet much too often we all find ourselves using words and phrases that our customers do not understand, which makes them uncomfortable.

Your goal as you do business is to make the customer feel "ok." You want to protect their ego at all costs. The quickest way to make them uncomfortable is to toot your horn and show how educated you are, which by default makes them feel like a child.

Take a moment and think about the last few customers you spoke with. Did you make them feel comfortable and welcome or did you show off your intellect and impress only yourself?

Chapter 30 – Creative Thinking

*C*reativity: the ability to transcend traditional ideas, rules, patterns, relationships, or the like, and to create meaningful new ideas, forms, methods, interpretations, etc.; originality, progressiveness or imagination.

Are you ready to try something different? Why not try some creative thinking?

Remember when you were in first grade and the teacher placed paper, paste and scissors on your table? You had no experience in the creative arts but that did not stop you from moving forward. Your work may not have changed the world but it was yours.

And it was an original.

Creativity and marketing

Turning your health department into a brand need not be difficult. In fact, it can be as fun as that first grade art project.

The first thing you need to try is having a childlike openness to your own ideas. As adults, we have spent many years being told, "no" or "that will never work" and what is terrible is that we believed it! Turn off those negative voices and tap into your creativity.

Step One

Take one service or benefit of your health department and write it in the middle of a blank sheet of paper. Draw a circle around it. Now draw five lines off the circle (like sun rays). At the end of those lines write words that describe the benefit you started with. Draw circles around those benefits with lines off of them and repeat the process.

Chapter 31 – New Technology

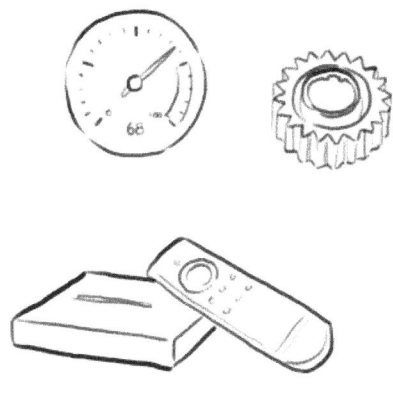

When Microsoft ceremoniously sent Windows XP to the digital graveyard, many businesses were sent into a spin. Why end such a great and trouble-free product? Was it money? Was it a need to be seen as a leader? Was it necessary? Yes, yes and yes.

Sometimes we find ourselves with new technology that causes us to cross into unfamiliar territory in hopes that it will make our lives better. Sometimes we go willingly and sometimes we are forced into updating.

New telephone system

With the advent of telephone systems with new features, such as auto attendant, voicemail and VOIP comes a need to move forward in more creative ways.

At Venue, we have helped many health departments with consulting (before the purchase of a new telephone system) as well as turning their new systems into a marketing goldmine.

The new technology doesn't end the need for professional marketing; it makes it more important than ever. For example, many of our customers now have us email their audio productions into their new system while others have us logon over the Internet to manage the way their system answers, what plays on hold and what callers hear after hours.

One health department recently benefited from our technology when we loaded an emergency message about TB on their phone system within 11 minutes!

If you are moving into a new phone system (or already have), let us help you make the jump easy, profitable and effective.

Chapter 32 – Anti-Vaccine War

What is behind the resistance to vaccine movement? Is it a bunch of holistic weirdos and conspiracy theorists or is there a breakdown in communication?

Not long ago, public health was seen as being at the forefront of fighting diseases that were killing children (and adults). With the polio and measles vaccine being a rite of passage for US children, we managed to eradicate these diseases. Parents weren't just supportive of vaccines for their kids, they were eternally grateful.

Today it is a different story. There are organized groups fighting hard to win the hearts and minds of parents in your community. Resistancemovement.org is a major player in the war against what they consider unnecessary vaccinations. They believe there is a coordinated effort by public health and pharmaceutical companies to create a culture of dependency on vaccine.

Where did this come from?

As far back as the late 60s, communes promoted what they believed to be a holistic approach to health. No meats, no processed foods, free love and limited exposure to our developed western culture.

At the same time, religious cults sprang up expounding the belief that God's children will need no medicine.

While it is not clear exactly where this current tide of anti-vaccine theory comes from, it is important that we educate our clients about the history of vaccines and how they have saved countless lives.

It may be time to counteract recent media exposure of this movement with education and a considerable effort at bridging the communication gap.

Chapter 33 – Creative Benefit Promotion

We live in a time when promotion is everywhere, anywhere and sometimes, nowhere.

Now that you have taken a creative look at some of the benefits your service offers, perhaps some new revelations are starting to emerge. Hopefully, you have developed a new idea or a new way of seeing where you fit in your marketplace.

How do you promote these new benefits?

Arriving on the scene in August of 2003, MySpace gave users a way to develop and promote a presence of the Internet without the need for a computer degree. Many adults (including myself) originally thought it was a place for kids to gather and connect. Boy, was I wrong!

Since 2003 we now have an unlimited amount of social media sites like Facebook, Twitter, Buzzfeed and more. There are even nightly reports on the news about what stories are "trending."

Not that social media is the only way to promote the benefits of doing business with you, but the benefits of social media marketing include:

1. Increased awareness of the organization
2. Increased traffic to website
3. Greater favorable perceptions of the bran
4. Able to monitor conversations about the organization
5. Able to develop targeted marketing activities
6. Better understanding of customers perceptions of their bran
7. Improved insights about their target market
8. Identification of positive and negative comment
9. Increase in new business
10. Identification of new product or service opportunities

11. Ability to measure the frequency of the discussion about the bran

12. Early warning of potential product or service issues

Now that we have defined some benefits and looked at social media, next we will look at creating your brand.

Time management and the myth of multi-tasking

Have you thought about how much time you spend doing activities that have zero payoff?

While in Japan in 2007, I noticed that everyone had their faces buried in their cell phones. In the States, we didn't have smart phones yet so this seemed extremely foreign. Passengers would board the train or subway and stare at their phones. It didn't take long for this time, wasting distraction to happen here!

The average teen sends 100 texts per day, (adults aren't much better)!

Our brains can only focus on one thought at any given time. Turning your cell phone on while reading email and focusing on your business just doesn't work.

Yet our brains have become addicted to the chemical rush we get when our cell phone buzzes with a text, a Facebook post or phone call. Attention spans and the ability to focus are disappearing.

How do you manage your time? Do you have a calendar on which you block out "pay-time" activities?

In 1971, Nobel Prize winner Herbert Simon wrote "In an information-rich world, the wealth of information means a dearth of something else: a scarcity of whatever it is that information consumes. What information consumes is rather obvious: it consumes the attention of its recipients. Hence a wealth of information creates a poverty of attention and a need to allocate that attention efficiently among the overabundance of information sources that might consume it." [9](ref-9)

If you would like to improve your personal productivity, try turning that cell phone off. Try scheduling your time, prioritizing things that improve your business, family or health. Focus on one thing at a time.

---

[9] *Ref 9*

Chapter 34 – Seven Ways Your Telephone System Torpedoes Your Success

You've done it! You finally have an effective marketing plan complete with a system to track your calls. Everything is falling into place but unless you address these shortfalls you are sunk:

1. The first impression/ the human factor - Why is it that the lowest paid, least trained person is the one charged with answering the phone? That's like hiring Bozo the Clown to be our Ambassador to the U.N.!

2. The first impression / the auto attendant factor - There's one thing everyone hates, having to weed through unprofessional sounding auto attendant prompts. "Thank you for calling....our menu has changed."

3. The endless phone tree - Most of auto attendant recordings are either recorded by the guy that installed your phone system or receptionist. Not very professional and what happens when they need to be recorded?

4. Unanswered calls going straight to voicemail - Statistics show that most callers hang up when confronted with voicemail. You've paid dearly to get people to call; now you've lost them without even talking to them. The potential lost opportunity cost can be staggering!

5. No on-hold marketing strategy- If your callers are listening to silence on hold, you might as well take up another vocation like parking lot attendant. Since the 1970s, callers have been conditioned to expect on hold messages while waiting to be helped. If you are playing nothing, they will think they got hung up on. If your competitors are playing on hold messages about

their business, how does that make you appear by comparison?

6. Speakerphones - You may think you're cool by using the speakerphone, but believe me, your callers don't. It is hard to understand.

7. After hours voicemail - Again, nobody likes to leave a voicemail. You have a captive audience just like on hold. Why not sell them something?

Chapter 35 – Flu Season = Sell Season

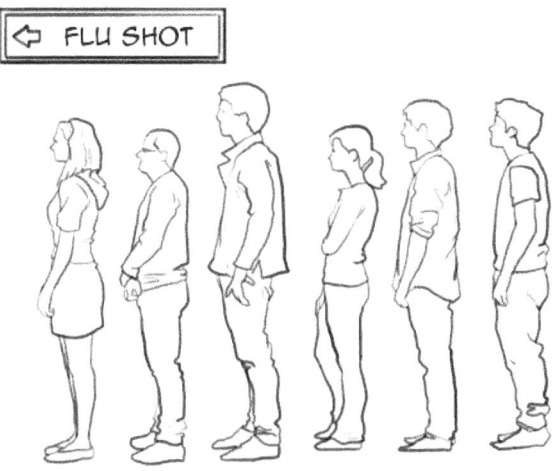

It happens every year:, kids go back to school, immunizations come in droves and flu season is right around the corner.

Each year health departments nationwide gear up to administer flu vaccines to millions and millions of recipients. Of all of the opportunities to make people aware of the services your health department provides, this is one of the best.

This year while your health department is bustling with the increased traffic of citizens seeking flu vaccine, why not take this wonderful opportunity and captive audience to share with them all of the services and programs your health department provides?

Just like McDonald's trying to upsell each drive-thru customer from a hamburger to a Big Mac, you can do the same thing with your health department for virtually no cost at all. Be prepared, have a clearly written brochure and train the staff to cross sell every single patient.

A wonderful idea is to track your results. How do you track results? One way is to put a little electronic stamp called a Quick Response Code that can be read by a smart phone that will instantly take your customers to a your website where you can track the results.

Small businesses have been using this technology for many years and it's time that health departments do as well. Software programs like Infusion enable you to track everybody that clicks on your website or email. What a wonderful way to build a brand, build excitement and increase traffic flow, all from cross-selling during flu season this year. Try it and you will be surprised!

Chapter 36 – 7 Reasons to Join a Mastermind Group

One of the most powerful tools available to anyone is joining a Mastermind group!

Mastermind groups are relatively new to most people, even though Napoleon Hill created the concept around 75 years ago with his book, "Think and Grow Rich." A Mastermind group is designed to help you navigate through challenges using the collective intelligence of others.

A Mastermind group offers a combination of brainstorming, education, peer accountability and support in a group setting to sharpen your business and personal skills.

Participants challenge each other to set powerful goals, and more importantly, to accomplish them. The group requires commitment, confidentiality, willingness to both give and receive advice and ideas, and support each other with total honesty, respect and compassion. Mastermind group members act as catalysts for growth, devil's advocates and supportive colleagues. This is the essence and value of Mastermind groups.

How does a Mastermind work?

A group of smart people meets monthly to tackle challenges and problems together. They lean on each other, give advice, share connections and do business with each other when appropriate. It's very much peer-to-peer mentoring and if you are lucky enough to get invited to one, you will most likely see a marked change in yourself and your business.

1. You'll be part of an exclusive community. The other members need you just as much as you need them, so quality of experience and knowledge is crucial to all involved.

2. Advisement. Once you are involved in a Mastermind, that feeling of "being alone" while running your business is gone. The other members of the group turn into business advisors of sorts and vice versa.

3. Collaboration is the name of the game. You may find someone in the group that is a perfect fit to work on a project with you. Or, you may be the perfect person to help another member as well.

4. Extend your network. By joining a Mastermind, you instantly add to your network and typically gain the networks of those in the group with you.

5. New learning. Everyone in the Mastermind is unique in skill, experience and connections. By interacting and sharing your challenges, it's almost certain that someone in your master-mind will have a solution for you and you may also be able to offer a solution, connection or tactic to help another in the group.

6. Cross-promotion. When you join a Mastermind, you will most likely find ways to help each other by utilizing cross promotion. Finding ways to help each other through promoting to your respective networks.

7. Think bigger. Being in a Mastermind will truly give you a Master Mind! You can't help but think bigger and stretch beyond your boundaries

when surrounded by amazing people doing amazing things.

Masterminds are incredible and can do wonders for your business as well as for you, personally. Growing in a group is not only more effective; it's quite a bit more fun!

Chapter 37 – Tracking Your Customer's Perspective

Previously, we talked about understanding the reality of how your customers see your business.

Anyone who has ever been on a cruise ship knows how dedicated the service staff are, especially room stewards and personal wait staff. On a recent trip, we had a room steward who immediately won us over with genuine humbleness and a ceaseless desire to please. Cruise ship employees are usually from 2nd or 3rd world countries and, as such, are not often paid very well. They make the bulk of their income from tips collected at the end of the cruise.

Our room steward shared with us that he had been working in the position for 12 years. When I asked how long before he retired, I assumed he would have a bright future. He said that in 10 more years he would retire and would receive a lump sum payment of $7,500!

What does this have to do with tracking your customer's perspective? Being that our steward gains most of his income from the meager tip he receives at the ends a trip, he truly needs to understand his customer's needs, anticipate their desires and be unfailingly prompt and courteous. If not, he gets immediate feedback and no tip.

Outside of immediate feedback how are we supposed to track our customer's perspective as they interact with us? How do you ensure they come back?

One way is to offer an affinity program. Affinity is that tight bond a customer has with a company and its brand. When a customer has affinity for your company, they're in a long-term relationship with you. Apple has it. ECCO has it. Polo has it. Coach has it. L.L.Bean has it. Mercedes-Benz had it and is working to gain it back (quality problems). Jet Blue had it and lost it (customers held on the tarmac). Natural Balance lost it (harmful pet food).

What is it like to buy your product? Is it being sold by a surly teenager, a condescending socialite or a passionate fan? Here are some ways you can provide a great buying experience.

Remember, customers have already made a commitment to you by making a purchase. Fail them when they need you to make it right and you've lost a customer—and 20 more when they tell their family, friends and the immediate world via their blog. As the old Texas saying goes, "You got to dance with them that brung you." Show some loyalty to the customers who brought you to this point in your company's evolution—they're the cause of your prosperity. Try to keep the customers who already love the service they're receiving and continuously fulfill the promise of your brand.

Chapter 38 – Retention: The New Acquisition

It's a well known fact that it is easier to keep an existing customer than it is to find a new one. In fact, it is four to 10 times more costly to find a new customer!

If businesses would take a portion of their marketing budget and put it towards existing client appreciation, their retention and revenues would increase. The statistic that I love is 68% of clients leave a business because they believe the business doesn't care about them. If you simply show your clients you care, you will retain that 68%.

One of the things we regularly do is help our clients understand that their customers don't know the other products and services they offer. We have multiple tools that do just that. From creating a direct marketing campaigns to referral coaching and messages that cross sell to every caller, we see it work every day.

Ride The Customer Engagement Cycle

To understand the concept let's look at what happens:

First they become your satisfied customer, then they are converted into a repeat customer through your appreciation of them and their awareness of what you offer. Then, through excellent treatment and ongoing care they return and also refer others.

If you would like help with turning your one-time customers into repeat customers who feel appreciated enough to return for your other products or services, call me.

Although your customers won't love you if you give bad service, your competitors will.

Chapter 39 – The Zika Virus / What Happened to Threat Preparedness?

Chicken Little said, "The sky is falling." Paul Revere said, "The British are coming." The difference between the two is while Revere had visual, unmistakable information to support his claim; Chicken Little was preparing the others for an unseen yet possible upcoming disaster.

Sound familiar?

Not long ago the public, the government and the media were all aware of how important threat preparedness was.

During the H1N1 situation every health department we work with was in dire need of targeted messages to inform the public about what was happening. The media loved the story about a possible plague and the government was doing its best to appear in control.

One of the services we provide health departments is our message on hold program. It was designed for just this type of emergency scenario. Our ability to make realtime, up to the minute changes to the messages callers hear while on the phone with the health department was put to good use.

For many years (since 9/11), emergency preparedness has been a big part of how we help. While many health departments split the cost for our marketing services between programs like WIC, family planning and clinical services such as immunizations and STDs, one of the most common has been threat preparedness.

Speaking with a public health director with 25 years experience, I was amazed at how she laid out the balance between public health and public awareness. She said, "That's the way it is in public health. Nobody thinks about us until there is a disaster."

Terrorism, ISIS, Mr. Jenner becoming Ms. Jenner and Donald Trump were all part of the crackling static we call media in 2015. Clearly, messages can become watered down when they are mixed in with gumbo that is competing with for your targeted audience's attention.

When a public health emergency suddenly arises, the seemingly important stories fade to the background.

Will the Zika virus be this year's H1N1? Will the EP see increased funding? Only time will tell but one thing is certain, as one of our customers, you can rest assured when the next crisis arises, we have your messaging covered.

Chapter 40 – Affordable Act Redefining Public Health

For many years, public health departments have offered a myriad of services as a safety net for people without insurance. From pediatric services to maternal health, family planning, immunizations and more, people knew they could count on the health department.

It seemed like a good idea at the time

Since passing the Affordable Care Act, I have spoken to numerous local health departments that have lost market share. They no longer have the menu of services they used to have. Many blame the ACA.

Silver lining?

As the smoke cleared, many realized the need to minimize lost opportunity and to become more creative in marketing their remaining services, seek new profit centers and to learn what others are doing to recreate the future of public health. There is an opportunity here, but it is going to take a commitment to marketing on a local level.

The days of passively waiting for the phone to ring or patients to walk through the door are over. Each local health department needs to reach out to their communities through marketing. By doing so, they will discover new needs and opportunity to expand their role instead of shrinking it.

Through marketing, creativity, partnering and a forward focus, public health can minimize the chaos and lost services caused by the Affordable Care Act.

Ask us how we can help with outreach, marketing and cross selling to your existing patients.

Chapter 41 – Keeping The Lights On

The pendulum of funding and budgets swings both ways. One period will see deep wells of money available while the next period sees an arid desert devoid of abundance.

"I was at a recent emergency preparedness summit and heard the same thing from several people, budget cuts resulting in staff layoffs," said Mike Hill a public health administrator and Venue client since 2000.

"I don't know how some are going to make it through this period. They don't have a marketing plan, they don't have the training. My education and background started in hospital administration where we embraced marketing. I don't think many schools offering degrees in public health focus on marketing."

Every week I speak with administrators who are seeking new ways to keep their health departments viable, to make due with less. While there are some who are frightened enough to cut programs and wave the flag of surrender, there are those that know they have to forget everything they thought they knew about marketing and start over seeking a fresh approach with our help.

My recent conversation with Mike Hill was enlightening. He is somebody who is not going to be happy with the typical marketing plan of using PSAs, newspaper blurbs or an occasional handout. "I don't know how some of my colleagues are going to make it", he said. "You have to keep the lights on. You just can't hope for one source of funding, you have to write grants, have a good relationship with your county government and seek creative ways to bring people in."

After my conversation with Mike I spoke with a public health director from another state who said she had a cut in funding and was fearful of having to layoff staff. After a long career in public health, she is set to retire in two months. Listening to her, I could sense the unfortunate sound of defeat in her voice. "The state wants us to bring in more primary care but local government wants to slash programs," she said.

When I shared that we have direct marketing programs that can reach every household in her county, that she could target specific neighborhoods that need the services of her health department the most, there was a long silence on the other end. "I didn't know you did that."

Today it's not just about keeping the lights on, it's about finding ways to bring in new clients while not competing with other providers. To do this you need to use the full arsenal of services we provide.

From workshops on new ways to market your health department to personal coaching and direct marketing campaigns targeted at specific neighborhoods and communities, ask us how we can help.

"From the early days back in 2000 I saw the benefits of your Call Handler program and how it delivered results to our health department," said Mike. "That's why I implemented your service in two of the states where I have served. It's not just about keeping the lights on."

Chapter 42 – What I Learned Crossing an Ocean

Recently I sailed 600 miles across the Gulf of Mexico with two retired psychotherapists. When making a long passage such as this, the three of us each had two hour watches where we were responsible for the boat and the lives of the other two.

You learn a lot about your fellow crew members on a long, non-stop sailing trip. There are hours and hours of conversation and these two gentlemen were a delight to talk to.

Inevitably, the conversation turned towards things we have accomplished and learned during our respective careers. While there were many metaphors and punch lines about, "I was sailing with two therapists when..." running through my mind, I found myself asking them what challenges they experienced trying to market the business of mental health.

One of the biggest issues they had to overcome was the public perception that mental health is only for crazy or sick people. They both wanted their communities to see mental health services as a normal and an everyday preventative health measure that just makes good sense. Everyone needs mental health services at one time or another.

Two approaches

While both came from the same industry (mental health), each had different methods of attracting new clients. Jay came from a social services background funded by his state while John came from a private practice background.

Jay said he had to constantly fight the stigma people had about mental health and that he could never find a way to break the barriers without being able to address them in a personal conversation.

John shared with me that the one thing he did that not only broke down barriers but bought in more clients than he could imagine was creating a newsletter that he sent to teachers, churches and other groups in his community. John's area of expertise was working with children and teens.

"Before long I started to grow my practice so much that I had to hire more staff just to keep up," he said. Eventually, I was asked to speak at a couple of psychology conferences about the successful marketing campaign I developed. From the podium, I would watch the faces of the attendees and could see that they were closed-minded about taking such an approach."

You can lead a horse to water..

Far from shore, there were hours and hours of interesting discussion. Everything from politics to sports, favorite movies, books we've read and even food. But the most enlightening was when I saw someone from a field as specialized as mental health experience achieve quantum growth by simply writing a bi-monthly newsletter.

As a client of ours, we can help you develop a newsletter campaign. Contact us for more help.

.

Chapter 43 – Putting It All Together

As we come to the end of the book, this is really just the beginning. Now it's time to take your health department to a whole new level. There is a difference. That difference is what we call transformation versus tweaking. What I've tried to accomplish with this book was to help you transform your health department's approach to marketing.

Small tweaks provide small results. Transformation is a brand new beginning. You have to have an absolute clarity about what you want, and what you're willing to do. You have to have a willingness to take total control of your daily behavior. Now is time to set specific goals and you will achieve them.

Please remember that "selling" is not a bad word. Selling is what you need to do to bond with your community to educate them about the services, and programs your health department has. Remember the tower of success and how imperative it is to go from level to level.

Following this program you've learned about the new paradigm, social media, and internet marketing. You've learned the most common mistakes public health departments make with their marketing. You've now had an opportunity to look and see lost opportunities, and what they cost you.

You have seen the benefits of partnerships, and how vital they are, and how by simply partnering with others, you maximize your efforts, and multiply the results exponentially. You've learned about direct response marketing, and how powerful, and affordable that can be. How you can tap into specific neighborhoods, specific socio-economic groups, ages, etc.

You've learned how powerful direct marketing can be, and how traceable the results are. You probably never said the words "cross-selling" until you read this book.

Now you know how viral cross selling is, and how there are so many lost opportunities as a result of not cross-selling every single customer your health department comes in contact with.

You've learned that money is truly not a major hurdle in marketing your health department. It just takes creativity, and a 100%, no holds barred commitment to doing whatever it takes to getting the job done. It takes following a plan. That plan is presented in the previous pages of this book. You've learned the power of call handling, and how amazing the results can be, when you merely up-sell every caller, or inform every caller of programs and services before the call gets to the receptionist. Powerful!

You've learned about ways others are providing impeccable, and memorable services to their clients. You've learned about the ways to get out of your comfort zone and out into the field while building the morale in your group. Going door-to-door, and how powerful that can be in marketing your health department.

We've learned about creating powerful, and succinct messages targeted to your particular market, and needs. You've learned about goal setting. Hopefully you have seen your staff, and your self from a different perspective that you've never considered. Maybe learned ways that you've made your clients or customers feel uncomfortable by using "work speak," or language that they do not understand.

You've learned about targeting your marketing towards the education, and communication level of the people that you're trying to work with. You've learned about creating affinity programs, and ways to create benefits that will create, and cause frequent visits from the same people. They will be able to enjoy all the services your health department provides.

You've learned of the seven ways that your telephone image torpedoes your health department's success, and how easy it is to fix any one of those. Now you can see that each season of the year annually has awesome marketing opportunities, such as flu season. When traffic at the health department is usually at an all time high. You've learned about the power of retention, and how vital it is to retain your customers. Knowing full well that the cost of attaining a new customer is much more expensive than keeping one that has already done business with you.

My goal with this book was to teach you ways to get off the hamster wheel and stop making the same mistakes over and over.

You have learned to create goals that are attainable in a step-by-step duplicable method of increasing awareness, prosperity, and abundance at your health department.

One last thing I'd like to say as we close the book. That's about wasting time. There are so many ways that people waste time within your health department. There are so many ways that your employees and staff can waste time when they need to be focusing 100% attention on growing your health department.

Those ways include cell phone addiction. For example, we know that when somebody gets a ding, or a vibration from their phone, it sends endorphins through their brain. It gives them a good feeling and makes them think, "Oh somebody's thinking about me, or I'm important." Turn your cell phone off while at work. Don't even have it on vibrate–it will do no good.

The next addiction is email addiction. Only check your email two times a day. Don't check it before 10 am. There's nothing that can't wait until after 10. When you open your email, you then become reactive instead of proactive. Let people know up front what your rules of engagement are. Tell them how you want them to communicate with you, and when you will return their messages. Meetings are another huge waste of time unless they have a written agenda, and a hard stop time.

Social media while being a very powerful marketing tool, is also a gigantic waste of time. My recommendation would be to tell your staff, unless that particular staff member is in charge of the social media marketing program, that none of the others are allowed to look at Facebook, or Twitter until after 5 o'clock. If they are caught doing it during hours, they should be fined or forced to sweep the floor!

I recommend that you teach your staff to only be on social media a maximum of 30 minutes a day. Even while at home. Another huge waste of time is the unscheduled inbound telephone calls. Unless you're expecting calls that are of a public health emergency nature, let them go to voicemail, or have your assistant answer the phone, and qualify whether or not these need to be answered today, or even tomorrow.

Lastly, I would say please don't waste any more time on unprofitable, unsuccessful, and meaningless marketing programs. In the previous pages of this book, I have laid out a step-by-step program for you to recharge your health department. To start a new day. To improve employee morale. To go from a small tweak to a complete transformation. Public health no longer needs to be on the shelf or in the closet.

Each and every one of you reading this book is a vital and important part of the public well-being. Please do not let anybody in local government let you think otherwise. Let's all work together, and take your health department from the best kept secret in the community to a vital, and respected center of influence and public health services today!

References

T-1 "This was their finest hour" is the title commonly attributed to a speech delivered by Winston Churchill to the House of Commons of the Parliament of the United Kingdom on 18 June 1940. Wikipedia

T-2 Dr. Gail Matthews is a clinical psychologist from Dominican University of California who has published a number of classic works that have gained international media attention. Dr. Matthews specializes in overcoming barriers to success and regularly lectures on Life and Behavioral Coaching, Positive Psychology. She has also conducted research studies into 'Imposter Syndrome.'

T-3 The Pareto principle (also known as the 80/20 rule, the law of the vital few, or the principle of factor sparsity) states that, for many events, roughly 80% of the effects come from 20% of the causes. ... Pareto developed both concepts in the context of the distribution of income and wealth among the population. Wikipedia

T-4 *The Laugh Model: Reframing and Rebranding Public Health Through Social Media*. Cameron Lister, Marla Royne, Hannah E. Payne, Ben Cannon, Carl Hanson, and Michael Barnes. American Journal of Public Health: November 2015, Vol. 105, No. 11, pp. 2245-2251. doi: 10.2105/AJPH.2015.302669

T-5 *You Can't Teach a Kid to Ride a Bike at a Seminar: Sandler Training's 7-Step System for Successful Selling* by David H. Sandler 1995 McGraw-Hill

T-6 *"The Importance of On-Hold Messages."* Anna Assad Houston Chronicle. Retrieved 14 February 2013. Wikipedia

T-7 *The Wizard of Ads: Turning Words into Magic and Dreamers into Millionaires*, Bard Press (June 2, 1998)

T-8 *The Devil in the White City: Murder, Magic, and Madness at the Fair That Changed America*, Erik Larson, Crown Publishers 2003

T-9 Herbert A. Simon, Wikiquote

Does Your Team Need Help?

Get the most impact from the concepts shared in this book by letting us help you:

Sales and Marketing Bootcamp

Rick will come to your health department and conduct a two-day sales and marketing bootcamp. Attendess will learn to use a set comprehensive marketing tools designed to help administrators and directors increase community awareness of their programs and services without all of the headaches that come from a lack of training and accountability. In this session you will learn the basics of creating and following a simple step-by- step marketing plan that will help your health department stop losing business to the competition while becoming impervious to budget cuts.

Ongoing Coaching

Everyone can benefit from ongoing coaching. Most concepts are forgotten after a few weeks. Coaching clients enjoy a system that "grows" people by enabling them to learn through guided discovery and accountability.

Team Seminars

Rick is available to come speak for your group delivering a sharing session designed to address the marketing issues your team faces.

Write to Rick at Venue, 8668 Navarre Parkway #103, Navarre, Florida 32566 or by email: rick@sellingpublichealth.com Call 877-773-9566